THE THIRD DIMENSION OF LITERACY

HOW TO BRING FILMMAKING AND MEDIA LITERACY INTO YOUR CLASSROOM

MEGAN KIEFER

THE THIRD DIMENSION OF LITERACY
HOW TO BRING FILMMAKING AND MEDIA LITERACY INTO YOUR CLASSROOM

Copyright © 2019 TakeTwo Film Academy.

All rights reserved. No part of this book may be reproduced in any form or by any electronic or mechanical means, including information storage and retrieval systems, without permission in writing from the publisher, except by reviewers, who may quote brief passages in a review.

ISBN: 978-1-951317-01-0

Editing by Weeva, Inc.
Cover design by Rachel Bostick of Weeva, Inc.
Book design by Cassidy Reynolds of Weeva, Inc.

Published by Weeva, Inc.
Austin, Texas
Visit weeva.com

"In an era of accelerating innovation...expanding our understanding of literacy isn't just important, it's essential to participating effectively and ethically in modern life. The Third Dimension of Literacy should be required for every educator in America and anyone else who cares about how we properly prepare the next generation to thrive in a world they're embracing faster than our teaching has up to now."

—Michael Slaby, Chief Strategist, Harmony Labs
(a non-profit focused on decoding the effects of media on society)

"The Third Dimension of Literacy" has taken the medium of filmmaking and turned it into a literacy. This book is a must have for teachers who are looking for a safe way to experiment with film and digital citizenship!"

—Ross Cooper, Author of Hacking Project Based Learning

"I had no idea how profoundly engaging film would be for my students. My ability to teach and theirs to grasp the content has expanded exponentially."

—Ellyn Lankford, 6th Grade Social Studies Teacher

"The benefit of this work is that it seamlessly integrates and supports the curriculum rather than adding an extra burden for teachers. For example, our second graders created outstanding bird documentaries as the culmination of our bird study."

—Pat Carney, Principal of PS 340

"This work was the perfect addition to our school. The impact and video work engaged our students and was invaluable in helping to solidify our students' learning. This work has now become embedded in the fabric of our culture."

—Jessica Jenkins, Founding Principal of the West End Secondary School

TABLE OF CONTENTS

PART 1 FUNDAMENTALS

13 CHAPTER 1 - WHAT IS THE THIRD DIMENSION OF LITERACY?

Understanding filmmaking as the next dimension of literacy; the Take Two Method for Project-Based Learning; and what to expect from this book.

27 CHAPTER 2 - PREPARATION

The importance of buy-in from administration; the equipment, software, and resources you will need and how to set up your classroom; and how to get your students organized and respectful for filmmaking.

43 CHAPTER 3 - LESSON PLANS

How to create customized lesson plans for both narrative/silent film and documentary film projects.

55 CHAPTER 4 - RESOURCES, SOFTWARE, AND SAFEGUARDS

Screenwriting and editing software options; understanding intellectual property, including where to find royalty-free resources for use in films; distinguishing between credible and non-credible sources; and a note on cyber-bullying.

PART 2 PRE-PRODUCTION

65 CHAPTER 5 - VIEWING: THE NEW READING

Passive versus active media consumption, and how to keep students engaged during viewings.

69 CHAPTER 6 - DOCUMENTARY FILM: THE NEW ESSAY

Understanding the different types of documentaries and the steps required to produce them, from creating your rubric to script-writing.

87 CHAPTER 7 - NARRATIVE AND SILENT FILM: THE NEW CREATIVE WRITING ASSIGNMENT

Understanding what makes a good narrative film and the steps required to make one, from storyboarding to screenplay.

PART 3 PRODUCTION

109 CHAPTER 8 - THE GRAMMAR OF FILMMAKING
How to use the grammar of filmmaking to get the right shot for the right moment and effect, including an educational production game.

115 CHAPTER 9 - DOCUMENTARY PRODUCTION
What it takes to produce a documentary film, from recording voice-over to recording interviews.

123 CHAPTER 10 - NARRATIVE PRODUCTION
A guide to student roles during production, including an educational game; and tips for shooting and for recording audio, and how to back up your students work.

PART 4 POST-PRODUCTION

131 CHAPTER 11 - EDITING
Key features of editing software; managing your class workflow; backing up data and watching dailies; and an overview of typical editing tools.

PART 5 MAXIMIZE YOUR IMPACT

143 CHAPTER 12 - SHARING AND COMMUNITY IMPACT
An overview of hosting your screening and the importance of sharing the film.

150 CLOSING THOUGHTS

152 GLOSSARY

FOREWORD

  I am an auditory and kinesthetic learner, which means that I struggled to learn to read and write. In the past, kids with challenges like mine were thrown into the classroom "pool" with ankle weights and had to outwork everyone else just to keep our heads above water. What I wouldn't have given for alternative ways of learning, such as YouTube tutorials or the ability to articulate my arguments in a documentary film rather than in an essay.

  I founded Take Two Film Academy in 2009 as a film school for children, teens, and young adults mostly because I liked making films and working with young people but also because I wanted things to be different and better for students like me—the students who use their ears and hands to learn and understand the world.

  Today, Take Two works within schools offering residency programs and after school programs, as well as running stand-alone workshops. Take Two student films are regularly screened at local festivals and have been a part of the Tribeca Film Festival since 2013. Our program has served hundreds of classrooms and thousands of students and now I am excited to bring it to you.

  What is this book about?

  I wrote this book as a way to codify and share our work with teachers and educators who might be inexperienced or insecure about working or teaching in this medium. Filmmaking and media comprehension is the literacy of the future and needs to be taught in schools as a way to meet young people where they are at and give them a framework for how to consume and create media ethically and responsibly. My hope for this book is that it encourages more teachers to adopt the third dimension of literacy and utilize it in all areas of study.

The book is meant to act as an introduction to the pedagogy of the third dimension of literacy and provide some basic "how-tos" on implementing it in your classroom. For additional resources we have created a Learning Management Site (LMS) to accompany this book. It provides coaching, rubrics, and more in-depth instruction on how to teach this material. I urge you to make use of the LMS just as fully as the text in this book Some techniques are best explained by a short video rather than by an extensive description. Sometimes video is simply better, which, of course, is the whole point.

—MEGAN KIEFER, PRESIDENT AND FOUNDER OF TAKE TWO FILM ACADEMY

DIGITAL FEATURES

Throughout the book, we have used QR codes to link to videos created by Take Two as well as resources that we have found to be particularly helpful in our teaching.

To access the resources, scan the QR code on the page using any QR-code scanning app. This will take you to the linked resource including the videos created by Take Two. On Vimeo, simply enter the password *taketwo*, press play, and watch. To access a full list of videos and resources, scan the QR code below.

Take Two resources.

PART 1
FUNDAMENTALS

CHAPTER 1
WHAT IS THE THIRD DIMENSION OF LITERACY?

"Literacy is the ability to read, write, speak and listen, and use numeracy and technology, at a level that enables people to express and understand ideas and opinions, to make decisions and solve problems, to achieve their goals, and to participate fully in their community and in wider society. **Achieving literacy is a lifelong learning process.***"*

—LITERACY ADVANCE OF HOUSTON[1]

Literacy is, and always will be, one of the prime responsibilities for educators. Typically we think about literacy as the ability to not only absorb the ideas of others (reading) but to communicate our own thoughts and ideas (writing). Now imagine that you were taught how to read but not how to analyze and deconstruct what you read. And more—that you were never taught how to write. You could absorb the ideas of others to some extent, but you could never really share your own. For as long as audio-visual media—including sound, video, and film—have been used in the classroom, this is what we've been asking our students to do. We expect our students to consume media passively without much analysis or deconstruction, and when we teach them how to make their own films we often do so without giving them any ethical guidelines for production. In today's media-driven landscape it is now more important than ever that we expand yesterday's definition of literacy to include the analysis and

---

[1] www.literacyadvance.org/About_Us/Defining_Literacy

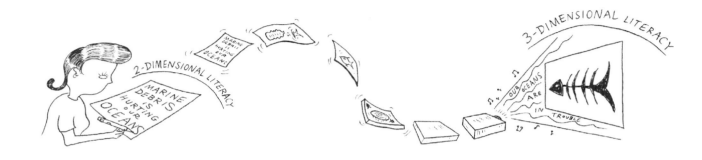

responsible creation of audio-visual media. We are calling this new literacy the third dimension: it now must include not only reading and writing text, but also understanding and creating audio-visual media.

LITERACY IS, AND ALWAYS WILL BE, ONE OF THE PRIME RESPONSIBILITIES FOR EDUCATORS.

THE THIRD DIMENSION OF LITERACY

Consider the first dimension of literacy a *word*, and the second dimension of literacy a *stringing together of words* to form a complete thought. The third dimension of literacy is *a visualization of a complete thought*: it takes those strung-together words and adds a sensory component using audio and video elements. So ***viewing* films and video becomes the third dimension of reading and *making* films and video becomes the third dimension of writing.** The classic essay transforms into a documentary film and the short story or creative writing project becomes a narrative/silent/experimental film.

This dimension is how our students are communicating today. They are doing it at home, but not in the classroom. This lack of interactivity is a huge missed opportunity and we must not only bring this third dimension into the classroom, but cultivate it to create a more literate population.

The next billion users of smartphones may not be traditionally literate, but you can bet that they will be third-dimensionally literate, communicating via video and audio much more frequently than we could ever imagine. Fluency in these mediums is no longer a "nice to have" skill for the future but a "must have." Businesses are looking for employees who are not only tech and computer savvy, but also for those who can communicate with customers in this multimedia world. Studies have shown[2] that when given the option between a written article or a video on the same subject, people will gravitate towards the video—another reason to become more literate in this space.

Medium Shot
(Sam looks up article online)

Close Up Shot
(Website offers written article and video)

Close Up Shot (Sam clicks on the video)

Close Up Shot (Sam is happy)

Medium Shot (Sam tells Jesse about what they just learned)

As educators, parents, and interested parties, it is now time for us to take on this new dimension of literacy and implement it effectively and responsibly in the classroom. Not only do we need to become skilled at teaching it, but teaching with it. This book will show you how to do it!

---

2 For example, see Liraz Margalit's article "Did Video Kill Text Content Marketing?", *Entrepreneur*, April 2016. www.entrepreneur.com/article/245003

THE STAKES ARE GETTING HIGHER

Across the country, more and more schools are starting to implement video into the classroom as a tool for learning, especially in schools that are implementing the flipped classroom, blended learning, and other experiential learning environments. Yet even in these classrooms, where students are interacting in three dimensions, they are still largely being taught literacy in two dimensions.

Think about the audience *reach* of an essay or creative writing assignment that a student completes. Typically, only the student's teacher and family would ever see it. Now, think of the potential audience *reach* for a video or piece of media that same student creates. That audience includes not just the student's class, but the whole school community—even the world (if the video goes viral). This medium can have enormous positive impact, and also has the potential to do a lot of harm. Treating this medium as a new level of literacy and creating a framework around how to interact with it at a young age is now essential. For example, we ask students to cite their work when they write a paper; we should be training them to do so when they make audio and video content.

When a student has made a mistake in an essay or there is misinformation in a writing assignment, the consequences are local. The teacher may simply put a red mark on the document and maybe deduct a few points. However, misinformation or inaccuracies in a documentary, Public Service Announcement (PSA), or narrative film that a student creates can ripple throughout the class, community, or whoever watches the film and trusts the creator to provide truthful content.

When video and media are integrated only as receptive tools and without giving students the chance to produce their own videos, this deprives the students of the ability to communicate effectively, powerfully, and ethically in this new world. Video production tools are no longer just for aspiring directors and producers. These are skills necessary in virtually every industry, across every sector of our economy.

While film and TV have been in the classroom for decades, the use has been one-way—as demonstrations or as substitutes for lectures. It is now possible and timely to use audio/video media not just as a means for creative artistic expression in art class, but also as a way of having students form and communicate their ideas in any subject in a way that goes beyond what is possible with reading, writing, or passively watching. On top of that, it offers a new instructional method for the teacher.

The Gallup Student Poll in 2015[3] surveyed students in grades 5-12 and found that 50 percent of students were either not engaged or actively disengaged in school. Meanwhile, most children get their first smartphone around age 10, and around one-third of U.S. students use tablets or other devices provided by their schools. We all know how engaged they are with those devices. While young people are using their smartphones or tablets for entertainment purposes they are not using them as educational tools. **As students learn how to create quality audio-visual media, they consume media more maturely and they hone the creative and analytical parts of their brain. This type of project-based learning helps with critical thinking as well as supporting personalized, tailored curricula for individual students.**

The technology for bringing video production into the classroom is more affordable and accessible than ever and we need to take the time and energy to integrate it.

---

[3] www.gallupstudentpoll.com/188036/2015-gallup-student-poll-overall-report.aspx

"Traditionally, producing, writing, and creating media has been viewed as elective education rather than a part of the core curriculum. Take Two Film Academy's approach is instead based on the assertion that: Creating video should be implemented into the traditional common core within all subjects."

THE TAKE TWO METHOD: PROJECT-BASED LEARNING

Traditionally, producing, writing, and creating media has been viewed as elective education rather than a part of the core curriculum. Take Two Film Academy's approach is instead based on the assertion that: Creating video should be implemented into the traditional common core within all subjects. The process we've developed to do so is a straightforward method that any dedicated teacher can use no matter what their level of experience or comfort with the technology.

Since our founding in 2009, Take Two has given more than 5,000 students a hands-on learning experience in a way that speaks to them and their interests, while introducing project-based learning and team-building at a very early age.

Here's what we've found in working with these students:

- Students feel engaged and excited when they work with video. Their enthusiasm increases, and their minds are more open to accepting and retaining new information. Assignments become fun.

- Students' desire to tell compelling stories and share information rises.

- Engaged students retain more of what they learn and retention levels increase after a student has produced a film or video.

- Editing, filming, and hands-on experiences give kinesthetic learners the chance to gain knowledge by seeing and interacting with a topic.

- Working with video gives auditory learners a chance to hear the content enough times that they can become experts in the unit they are studying.

- Watching and rewatching a film or project gives visual learners a chance to see what they are learning multiple times so they retain more information.

- Producing a video reinforces students' respect for one another and their work, the school equipment they are excited about using, and the intellectual property of others.

- Students learn to distinguish between credible and non-credible sources.

- Students increase their ability to think analytically.

Imagine a video-focused classroom where students are shown an interview from an "expert" who claims there's no proof that human activity is leading to more species of animals becoming extinct. Students analyze this expert's main points, and conduct research to discover alternative points of view. Perhaps they even conduct some primary interviews themselves! They film their rebuttal, using their filmmaking skills to convey a thoughtful, well-reasoned argument in a persuasive and appealing style, with visuals and archival footage that

bolster their argument. In the 20th century such an activity would have taken the form of a five-paragraph essay. In the 21st century, it can be accomplished with immersive filmmaking. With this video, education doesn't have to stop when the project is complete. There are multiple platforms where students can share their learning and continue their engagement.

WHAT TO EXPECT FROM THIS BOOK

The techniques in this book can sound formidable, but when implemented, you'll find them to be straightforward and fun, not only for your students but for you as well. This book will provide you with a toolkit to implement the Take Two Method in your classroom. You will learn:

- How to choose which unit of study will be appropriate for the kind of project you want to conduct and how to decide between making a documentary or narrative style film with your students.

- How to have conversations and analyze existing media within that subject, then prepare students to create their own films.

- How to have students implement their own findings into a video version of the traditional five-paragraph essay or creative writing assignment by teaching pre-production, production, and post-production for both narrative and documentary film.

- How to safeguard against unreliable research and cyber-bullying.

- How to source royalty-free music and other intellectual property without infringement.

- And lastly, how students can continue their educational journey by sharing their video to create an impact with a call to action.

SPEAKING OF CALL TO ACTION

As a society we need to start to look for more opportunities to integrate film and video into the core curriculum of schools. Why? Because media literacy has become essential to modern life.

Students love the power of images and love seeing themselves on film (for the most part). This is *their* literacy. They want to share their ideas with the world. When we teach media literacy, we're giving them the power to shape their own futures while promoting engaged learning. You only need to look to the growing popularity of YouTube tutorials and video lectures to see just how effective video can be as a learning tool. As more and more schools adopt flipped classrooms, blended learning, or other project-based learning experiences for their students, there will be many more opportunities to integrate media literacy into curricula.

IT'S ABOUT UNDERSTANDING THE LANDSCAPE OF WHERE YOU ARE AND WHERE YOU WANT TO BE, WITHIN THE CONTEXT OF THE SCHOOL'S POLICIES.

CHAPTER 2
PREPARATION

Getting ready to teach always requires preparation. In the case of teaching filmmaking you will need buy-in from your administration, specific equipment, and different classroom management skills. This chapter provides you important organizational information. Filmmaking in the classroom is not difficult to teach, but the set-up and preparation is essential for success.

BUY-IN FROM ADMINISTRATION

Ideally your administration is supportive in this endeavor and, like you, will want to showcase your students' work on classroom walls or on digital bulletin boards. Every school's culture is different when it comes to handling media. Some schools have their own YouTube channel, some schools don't; some schools have families sign media release forms and others don't. A lot depends on the environment of the school.

If your school has a YouTube channel—great! Use it. If it doesn't have a channel, consider creating one or share your students' films privately using an online sharing platform. Utilizing YouTube is more for a learning moment and not for the expectation that the film will go viral. Note that we've never had an issue posting content on YouTube; if we did, we'd simply take the materials down. We *have* had experiences where a parent might say, "I don't want my kid on YouTube," which is fine. Then we just take the video down and share the videos with password protection in Google Docs or Vimeo.

You should also have a permission slip that includes video (especially if a student's image will be on film). A lot of schools have these in place already, outlining who is allowed to be filmed and who is not allowed to be filmed. And just because someone can't be filmed doesn't mean they can't participate; there are many behind-the-scenes roles a student can take.

When you're talking to the administration, find out what the culture is when it comes to sharing videos online. Is it preferable to share via Google Drive or Dropbox or YouTube? Can materials be shared just with your class, or also with teachers and families in the school community? Or do you want to put the videos out on the Internet and see where they can go? Every school is different. Every parent is different. It's about understanding the landscape of where you are and where you want to be, within the context of the school's policies.

> *"...Just because someone can't be filmed doesn't mean they can't participate; there are many behind-the-scenes roles a student can take."*

AS YOUR FILMMAKING PROGRAM GROWS

If you start to develop a bigger film program within your school, you may need or want to purchase equipment (e.g., higher-speed computers for video editing, better cameras, audio equipment, steady cams, etc.) or hire an in-house film teacher who can monitor equipment and do a deeper dive into teaching the grammar of film. Better equipment will allow your students to create more interesting special effects, achieve higher production value, and better sound. While students can get quite excited about advanced technology it's not necessary to have, especially for academic purposes.

If your school doesn't have the budget to hire an in-house film teacher there are also many filmmakers out there who would be thrilled to come in and share their knowledge with students. A visiting expert discussion could be on anything from how the filmmaker chooses shots to how to create world-changing documentaries. There are many wonderful opportunities to integrate filmmaking and storytelling into your school and into your curriculum.

PRO TIP! DEPUTIZE YOUR CLASSROOM FILMMAKER

If your school can't hire a film teacher, keep in mind that for your students, this is already their language; we're the ones catching up. There will always be those few kids in the classroom who are just a little further along (maybe further along than you). Maybe they have their own production studio at home. Maybe they've got their own YouTube channel. Maybe they've already played around with editing. Consider deputizing these students to be co-teachers with you and enable them to answer other students' questions during class.

Leaning on your students can also be a good way to deal with behavioral issues in your class. There will always be "that" student, and they will pull focus away from the task at hand, impeding the progress of other students if the issue isn't dealt with properly. Something shifts for a person when you deputize them (especially if they

AFTER STUDENTS ACQUIRE A NEW SKILL, THE GOAL BECOMES ENCOURAGING **THEM** TO BE TEACHERS, HELPING OTHER STUDENTS IN THE CLASSROOM.

seem to be the source of a lot of the behavioral issues in the classroom) and give them responsibility, particularly when you're doing something very kinesthetic, very hands-on, very project-based. Now the student who was once disruptive will be the one saying, "Guys, come on, we've got to do this," becoming a leader instead of a disruptor.

For example, in one Take Two classroom, we had a student whose behavior prevented her group from getting their work done, sometimes influencing the productivity of the class as a whole. Then we sat down with her and showed her a bunch of editing tricks. She got really excited. Next, we had her teach everyone else. She walked around the room and helped all the other kids get their films done, accelerating productivity instead of detracting from it.

After students acquire a new skill, the goal becomes encouraging *them* **to be teachers, helping other students in the classroom.**

PREPARE TO TEACH

Before introducing filmmaking to your students, you yourself should be reasonably comfortable with the tools, resources, and processes that lie ahead, and have ensured that your classroom is set up to facilitate the unique needs of filmmaking.

Select sharing technology. It's really helpful for students when they're collaborating to use a productivity tool like Google Docs that enables sharing. This way they can interact with each other during every stage of the project, whether that means doing research for the documentary or writing scripts for the narrative. If your school is not set up with Google Classroom, or the equivalent, then sharing will be more challenging. However, you can still use group folders and stick to the pen and paper method for research and script-writing.

Organize production equipment. If students are going to be shooting a film, you want to make sure they have access to a video recording device, like an iPad, phone, or camera. Handheld consumer devices have come a long way in terms of video quality, and because your students have most likely handled one before your project, they will quickly adapt to shooting. This sort of device also allows you to quickly and easily back up footage to a drive or laptop. Any type of video recording camera will work, but you want to make sure that your students have access to editing software as well. We recommend that there is one recording device and two editing stations per group. Typically you want your students to be in groups of three to six (depending on the project, the size of the class, and how well your students work together). So, if you have a class of 30 you should have six or seven recording devices, and ideally twelve editing stations.

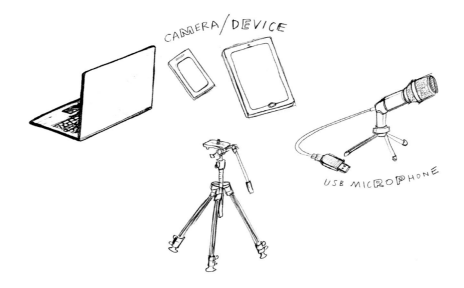

Select editing software. When Take Two was founded in 2009, YouTube was hardly "a thing." Ten years later we can upload terabytes of media into the cloud and edit it using high-speed Internet. Editing can feel somewhat intimidating if you are new to it, but there are a wealth of tutorials online if you or your students ever get stuck. People are always coming out with great ways to help you find shortcuts or do the exact thing you want to do online. Selecting your software is also a great opportunity for you to ask your students what they use to make their videos at home, because this is what they're doing! Alternately, you may just have to use what is accessible to you and your school.

There are many different types of editing software out there, such as: iMovie, which comes free on Apple devices; Windows Media Player, free on Windows computers; and WeVideo, which is a really great way of collaborating (it's almost like Google Docs for video editing). If you want to get a little more advanced or if your school has the budget, you could consider investing in professional-grade software such as Final Cut Pro or Adobe Premier. (See Chapter 4 for more on all of these.) But this is an industry where the technology is changing fast and professional features migrate to the free consumer-grade software very quickly. The latest, most powerful technology isn't required for your purposes. Again, this is a great opportunity to ask your students what they use. At the end of the day, you really want to be asking yourself: How can I support my students in making sure that the material and information they put into their films is effective, responsible, and entertaining? This all happens in the Edit, which we will cover extensively in Chapter 11.

Use online resources and tutorials. YouTube tutorials are huge, and luckily, it's a medium that your students are very used to. Even seasoned industry experts use tutorials—in an industry that changes so quickly, there's always a new piece of software or a new technique to learn. There's a whole network of wonderful people who are actively and freely sharing knowledge and information.

> *"It's A-okay to be an amateur!"*

Never underestimate the power of a basic Internet search. Want to learn how to reverse a clip in iMovie? Google "how to reverse a clip in iMovie." Each software program has its own set of shortcuts, most of which you or your students can learn with the help of a two-minute video, becoming a better, faster editor along the way. The same goes for shooting, doing interviews, three-point lighting systems, and the 180-degree rule. The skills that filmmakers go to NYU film school to learn are all online!

Remember: It's A-okay to be an amateur! The more you do as an amateur, the better you get at storytelling, and with today's production methods, you can learn very quickly. That's all part of the process of understanding the third dimension of literacy.

Enlist student help. Unfamiliarity seems to be what keeps teachers from doing this work in their classroom. It's new, and the idea of teaching something new can be daunting. But recognize that your students do this all the time and lean on them: let them teach you. This is a great opportunity for you to promote student agency and engagement around what you're teaching them. Plus, it's really exciting and fun when you can learn from your students.

Allot time. While you are lesson-planning, allot enough classroom time for students to work and make their films together. You want classroom time to be spent *making*, which promotes engagement and gets your students excited about what they are learning. Your classroom will start to feel like a mini-production studio.

PREPARE THE ASSIGNMENT

Shape the topic. The first thing you want to do is pick the area of study for your project, and wherever possible, integrate it into the overall curriculum. For example, we worked with a group of sixth graders who were studying the hero's journey in English, ancient Egypt in Social Studies, and microbial diseases in Science. Their film assignment had to take place in ancient Egypt, the protagonist had to struggle with a deadly microbial disease, and they had to incorporate five components of the hero's journey within their films. It was incredible!

In another example, we worked with a group of second graders while they were studying birds in the springtime. Each student was assigned a bird. They sparkled with enthusiasm as they researched their bird, writing down notes in their research folders like: "The bluebird is a very aggressive bird." Once their research was complete, we worked with each student to individually help them create a script about their bird, which we recorded, and then helped them to pick images to go along with their voice over. The students loved it because they got to hear their own voices, do their own research, pick their own images, and edit their own films.

Preassign groups. We recommend dividing students into groups of three to five people, especially if you have a larger class of 30 or more, and then creating shared Google folders for each team. Smaller groups allow the students not only to populate the folders with their research and documents, but to see what the other people in the group are finding and contributing. It creates a fun, almost poster board-like quality to the lesson, except it's all in the digital cloud. If you are utilizing group folders then still make sure that the individuals in the teams are collaborating and working together, sharing the workload.

Decide film type. You need to decide if you are going to have your students make narrative or documentary films, and if you are letting students pick the topics of their films or if you are assigning topics. If you want to make something more research-focused then Documentary is likely the best fit. If you want to do something more creative then Narrative is the way to go. Say you are teaching the Revolutionary War in class and you want your students to strictly report on the facts of the Boston Tea Party. Make a Documentary. However, if you would like them to create reenactments or historical fiction about the Boston Tea Party, then Narrative film would be a better choice. Take Two's Learning Management System (LMS) provides examples of the different tracks and includes downloadable lesson plans for the different types of film projects.

Watch examples of film type. We'll go over this in more depth in Chapter 5, but it's always good to show an example of the type of film you are about to make with your students so that they can see what the end results might look like. This is also a good opportunity to start the conversation on how to analyze film and breakdown production and story elements.

Plan for assessment. Before you start your project you will also want to create a rubric (for samples, see Chapters 6 and 7). The rubric is to help you assess your students' understanding of both the academic material they are learning and the literacy of

4   Intro Video.

film. While obtaining the skills and understanding the craft of filmmaking is terrific, it's even better if they can use these skills to create engrossing and content-driven movies.

CLASSROOM MANAGEMENT

Dedicated computer area. Try to create a dedicated area in the classroom for students to set up computers, a place where, for example, you might say, "Now we're going to work on editing," or, "Now we're going to work on your screenplays." You want to set up your classroom to make sure transitions are easy and seamless by using learning stations, rotation models, and computer carts. In most cases, you can use your existing system for student-technology interaction.

Signaling attention. Make sure you have set up your classroom management style for signaling attention. Filmmaking will be a messy (and loud) business at times. You need to be able to call everyone back together in order to maintain a respectful environment.

Share ideas. A lot of students are initially reluctant to share their ideas. They think their idea might not be good enough. They think they might be put down by their classmates. We try to encourage and promote one goal: to create a really great film. You can't have a really great film without everyone sharing their ideas. Even if a student thinks no one will like his or her idea, the act of sharing (even if it's under-developed) can inspire other people into speaking and sharing their thoughts. And we have seen many times that one idea from a quiet kid redirects an entire movie.

To help break the ice, we often go around the room and let everyone share one idea at a time. If the students have new ideas while they're listening to others, we encourage them to write their ideas down versus blurting them out; that way, when it's their turn again, the student has some new ideas to share.

Give and show respect. Of course you have your own way of managing your classroom. But we do want to highlight that in a collaborative, creative process, it's very important to reinforce good decorum and respectful behavior.

"Give and show respect."

Respect is not only important in the classroom, with teachers and classmates, but also in the entertainment industry. Teaching how to give and show respect in creative group work is an important life skill, and by enforcing it with this project your students will learn how to behave in that way across all the other parts of their lives.

At Take Two we promote four pillars of respect:

1. **Creativity**: Teach students to value everyone's creative input. Remember, every single idea is a good idea. Ensure your students respect their own ideas and those of their peers. Teach them to avoid the word "no" in a creative atmosphere because it shuts down productivity and creativity. Instead, they should use language like "yes, and" and "how about?" in order to provide constructive criticism. Putting anyone down is completely unacceptable and not tolerated.

2. **Equipment**: Show your students how to care for all of the special, expensive, and fragile equipment they're using.

3. **Space**: Encourage them to honor the space in which they've been given permission to create and film. We call it "leave no trace" filmmaking: every space and room in which we film should be left better than we found it.

4. **Time:** Show them how to leverage each and every minute of their filmmaking time.

When we respect these four pillars (creativity, equipment, space, and our time), we set ourselves up to make awesome films. When we don't, it inescapably shows in the work.

SUMMARY

- **What you'll need:**
    - Buy-in from administration.
    - Devices or cameras for filming: at least one camera for every five students.
    - Computers with editing software: at least one computer for every two or three students.
    - Sharing software, such as Google Docs, for easy sharing and collaboration.

- **Things to consider:**
    - While you, as the educator, may not be fully comfortable in the language and grammar of filmmaking, your students are using it in their daily lives. Lean on them.
    - Be patient with yourself as you experiment with integrating filmmaking into your classroom. As with anything else, there is a learning curve.
    - Spend some time getting comfortable with the equipment and tools you select.
    - Familiarize yourself with all available resources (see Chapter 4).
    - Encourage students to teach each other.

- Remember, if you or they get stuck, YouTube tutorials are your friends!
- Make sure you have set up your classroom effectively and don't forget to include a system for signaling attention. Filmmaking is a noisy endeavor and needs a disciplined classroom.

- **Once you're ready:**
  - Pick an area of study that can easily be presented using either documentary or narrative film.
  - Prepare a lesson plan (see Chapter 3).
  - Set up dedicated areas in the classroom for computers.
  - Show a video to prepare for the work ahead that can also act as an example of the type of film you wish students to make.
  - Remind students that showing respect is essential for successful filmmaking.
  - Respect each other (teachers, peers, yourself).
  - Respect every idea. Use supportive language like "yes, and" and "how about?" Avoid "no" and "but" as they close ideas down.
  - Respect the space you're in.
  - Be respectful of the computers and the equipment. Treat the equipment even better than your own possessions.
  - Respect the time available for work.

CHAPTER 3
LESSON PLANS

What are your students currently learning in school, and what would you like them to get out of your film project as it's integrated into the overall curriculum? This chapter provides tools to help you select between a Documentary or Narrative film and then shows you how to structure and prepare to launch the project. It includes detailed lesson plans and links to instructional Take Two videos for both Documentary and Narrative films.

HOW TO CHOOSE DOCUMENTARY OR NARRATIVE FILM

Documentary films are great for research and sharing information, while Narrative films allow for a more creative way to explore topics. For example, a science class could be learning about notable women in physics and a short, biographical documentary about each figure could replace or augment your typical essay assignment. Or if a class is reading a novel in English, students could create a movie sequel to explore what the characters would do after the book has ended.

While the possibilities are unlimited you should be sure to take into account the amount of time you have for this project: Documentaries are a little less time-consuming than Narratives. Your physical surroundings may play a part in what you can create. For example, if your school is next to a noisy construction zone, you may want to make a silent movie with title cards instead of trying to record audio.

The following lesson plans are to help you plan once you have read the rest of the book, all the lessons refer to forthcoming chapters in pre-production, production and post-production—we will not be going in depth on what you will be teaching here.

LESSON PLAN FOR NARRATIVE FILM (8-15 CLASS SESSIONS)

TYPICAL CLASS PERIOD: 50 MINUTES

PRIOR TO CLASS - EVERY CLASS (10 MINUTES)

Set up your classroom. Check that all computers work and have access to editing software and online collaboration platforms. If you have access to a smartboard or projector for showing examples, make sure you can connect.

Maintain your classroom protocol. The filmmaking component should fit within your typical routine for starting class.

CLASS 1: CREATING STORY STRUCTURE

1. INTRODUCE STORY STRUCTURE (15 MINUTES)

Go over story structure and if possible show some examples of short films. For a list of movies that illustrate structure, visit our Learning Management System (LMS) site. After viewing, ask the students:

- To describe the Beginning, Middle, and End (BME) of the story.
- What were the Five W's (who, what, where, when, and why) addressed in the beginning of the movie?
- What types of characters were represented in the film?
- What was the protagonist's goal and what were some obstacles to achieving it?

2. INTRODUCE THE CLASS ASSIGNMENT (5 MINUTES)

Introduce the project. For example, let's say that the students have been reading *To Kill A Mockingbird* by Harper Lee and that the project is for groups of students to create a short film about a specific character that takes place five years after the events of the book.

3. ORGANIZE GROUPS (5 MINUTES)

Once the assignment is clear, place students in filmmaking groups of four to six; try to design the groups based on who will work well together. Then (continuing our example) assign each group a specific character to base their story on. Choices might include Scout, Jem, Dill Harris, Boo Radley, or Mayella Ewell.

4. CREATE STORY ARCS (REMAINDER OF CLASS)

On paper, students should come up with their BME, write out their story arc, and start to answer the Five W questions. Using the protagonist they were assigned, ask them to imagine where their character is five years after the conclusion of the book. They should identify a goal for this character and some obstacles to place in their way. By the end of class students should have a rough draft.

CLASS 2: OUTLINES AND SCRIPTS

1. REVIEW STORY STRUCTURE (10 MINUTES)

Go over the elements of story structure again. (The Take Two video "Story"[5] provides a short, comprehensive overview.)

2. COMPLETE STORY ARC AND OUTLINES (REMAINDER OF CLASS)

Or until the class is finished outlining. If you have more time, you can introduce screenwriting.

Have the teams continue to work on their outlines. Explain that once the outlines are completed, they will move on to scripts.

5   Take Two Film Academy video tutorial, "Story."

3. WRITE SCRIPTS[2] (25 MINUTES)

Introduce how to write scripts. Use the smartboard if you want everyone to watch at the same time, or Google Docs if you want students to watch the video as they are ready. Invite students to begin writing their own scripts. Make sure they are sharing the document with you so you can monitor progress and add notes.

6 Take Two Film Academy video tutorial, "Script Writing."

CLASS 3: FINISH SCRIPTS AND EDITS

1. CONTINUE TO WRITE SCRIPTS (25 MINUTES)
Review how to write scripts. Have groups continue to work on and refine their script using Google Docs or similar sharing software. Make sure they continue to share the document with you so you can monitor progress.

2. READ SCRIPTS ALOUD (25 MINUTES)
Read the scripts aloud as a class. Jot down any and all changes that students suggest. Remember that since this is their creation, they should all be happy!

3. EDIT SCRIPTS (REMAINING CLASS TIME, OR AS HOMEWORK)
Have students finalize the scripts based on class feedback.

CLASS 4: CASTING, STORYBOARDING, LOCATIONS, AND FILMING

1. OVERVIEW AND CASTING (15 MINUTES)
Review the Take Two video "Actors, Locations, and Storyboarding."[7] Then have the teams cast their video.

2. STORYBOARDING AND LOCATIONS (15 MINUTES)
Have the students also divide the script so everyone is in charge of storyboarding at least one scene, and have them pick the location for that scene.[8]

2. REVIEW FILMING PROCESS (15 MINUTES)
Show the Take Two video "Shooting"[9]

3. FILMING (REMAINDER OF CLASS)
Start shooting.

CLASS 5 OR 5-10: PRODUCTION

1. FILMING (ENTIRE CLASS TIME)
Allow students class time to film their projects. If they need more time, assign it as homework.

7 Take Two Film Academy video tutorial, "Story."

8 Take Two Film Academy video tutorial, "Actors, Locations, and Storyboarding."

9 Take Two Film Academy video tutorial, "Shooting."

CLASS 6 OR 11-14: POST-PRODUCTION

1. PREPARING TO EDIT (20 MINUTES)
Review the Take Two video "Editing"[10] with your students at the start of class.

2. EDITING (REMAINDER OF CLASS)
Let students edit their films.

CLASS 7 OR 15: SCREENING DAY

1. HOST SCREENING DAY (ENTIRE CLASS PERIOD)
Show the films. Let students introduce the film and, at the end, invite them to describe the most fun and most challenging aspects of producing their film.

10 Take Two Film Academy video tutorial, "Editing."

LESSON PLAN FOR DOCUMENTARY FILM (7-10 CLASS SESSIONS)

TYPICAL CLASS PERIOD: 50 MINUTES

PRIOR TO CLASS - EVERY CLASS (10 MINUTES)

Set up your classroom. Check that all computers work and have access to editing software and online collaboration platforms. If you have access to a smartboard or projector for playing examples, make sure you can connect.

Maintain your classroom protocol. The filmmaking component should fit within however you choose to start each class.

CLASS 1: TURNING AN ESSAY INTO A FILM

11 Take Two Film Academy video tutorial, "Documentary."

1. EXPLAIN PROCESS FOR MAKING DOCUMENTARIES (20 MINUTES)
Watch different types of documentaries. Explain the basic structure of how to turn an essay into a documentary.

2. ORGANIZE GROUPS (10 MINUTES)
Put students in filmmaking groups based on what film they want to make. Try to design groups based on who will work well together.

3. OUTLINE STRUCTURE OF THE FILM[11] (REMAINDER OF CLASS)
Have students create a Google Doc with the structure of their documentary.

CLASS 2: WRITING

1. SCRIPT WRITING (ENTIRE CLASS)
Continue to have the students write scripts in groups. You can either write the scripts with them using the smartboard so they can all watch, or if they are literate have them write their scripts using Google Docs. Make sure they are sharing the document with you so you can monitor progress and provide feedback.

CLASS 3: TABLE READS/VOICE OVERS (VO)

1. READ SCRIPTS (20-30 MINUTES)
Go over scripts and read them aloud. Jot down any and all class suggestions. Have small groups consider and either accept or reject each change. Remember this is their creation, they should all be happy!

2. RECORD VOICE-OVERS (TIME VARIES)
Start to pull groups out of the room to start recording their voice-overs. Make sure to find a quiet place to do this.

CLASS 4: FINALIZE VOICE-OVERS

1. FINISH RECORDING VOICE-OVERS (ALL OF CLASS)
If your students finish early, have them start to look for music, B-roll, or other graphics for their films. Sometimes we also have students create posters for their films if they have extra time.

CLASS 5: PRODUCTION/EDITING

1. SHOOTING INTERVIEWS (20 MINUTES)
Explain how to shoot interviews.

2. PULLING B-ROLL (30 MINUTES)
Explain how to pull B-roll (archival footage, images, or videos that support what they are saying).

CLASSES 6-10: POST-PRODUCTION

1. EDITING (ENTIRE CLASS PERIOD)
Let students edit their films.

CLASS 7 OR 11: SCREENING DAY/ LAST DAY

1. HOST SCREENING (ENTIRE CLASS PERIOD)
Show the films. Invite students to introduce their films, and then discuss the filmmaking process afterward.

SUMMARY

We will go into much greater detail as the book progresses, but after reading this chapter you should now have a basic understanding of what it takes to create a lesson plan for both Narrative and Documentary film projects with your class.

CHAPTER 4

RESOURCES, SOFTWARE, AND SAFEGUARDS

Guiding you in this endeavor are several resources that are available for free or for a low cost on Take Two Film Academy's website (taketwofilmacademy.com), Take Two's LMS,[12] and across the Internet. As technology is always changing, it's best to check online for the latest and cheapest options before you begin. It's also a great opportunity to ask your students what they are using at home. This chapter will outline royalty-free resources, software options, and safeguards while navigating online content.

12 Take Two's LMS.

ROYALTY-FREE RESOURCES

When making films with your students they may not have time to shoot all of the principal photography, create all their own B-roll (overlaying images and video), or write their own music. Finding and using royalty-free images, music, or video is a great way to increase the production value of your students' films. YouTube is a great resource for filmmakers; you just have to know what to search for. If you're doing a documentary on the migration habits of cardinals and you simply do a search for "cardinals," you'll probably end up with thousands of old baseball clips. Make sure your search terms are as specific as possible. To find good B-roll and archival footage, try including the terms "stock footage" or "copyright free."

Also keep an eye out for video quality: ideally you'll want videos at a nice crisp 1080p resolution or at least 720p. For archival footage (e.g., from an old TV show), this is less important. When doing a search you can filter by video quality so that you only get HD video results or by upload date. Remember the early days of YouTube? Their video compression was pretty rough so you might want to skip using video created before 2010.

YouTube is also an excellent place for special effects and music. Many content creators will upload graphics with a green background that can be keyed out when imported into your movie. If you want a magical effect in your movie you could search for "green screen smoke puff." There is a whole channel called the Audio Library[13] that is devoted to free-for-use background music. It even has playlists based on musical style and mood, though it is very contemporary-sounding and may not be the place to go for your documentary on the Great Depression. The Audio Library has download links for each track.

You will need a third party program to download other video files: some options are yout.com, youtubetomp3, and Quicktime. Other great resources for copyright-free or fair use video and audio are creativecommons.org and archive.org (the latter leans towards older media).

13 Audio Library.

You may also find yourself looking for still images; in this case, Google Images is your friend. Again, try to keep your searches specific. "Cardinal bird close up" will give you better results than "cardinals." When doing an image search, make sure to hit the tool selection, go to size, and select "Larger than 2 MP." This will ensure that your photo won't look blurry next to your nice HD video. To ensure that the image isn't copyright protected you can click on Usage Rights and select "Labelled for reuse with modification." To download photos you can left click (for PC) or control click (for Apple) on the image and select "Save image as."

SCREENWRITING SOFTWARE OPTIONS

Following is a list of some free and paid screenwriting software options. We recommend using free whenever possible and we tend to use Google Docs the most for writing, mostly for its ease of use and classroom management components. If your school really gets into creating a robust film program you can upgrade to more sophisticated software options. Writing programs are usually very affordable; even the paid options below rarely exceed $100.

- Adobe Story (https://story.adobe.com): Low monthly subscription
- Amazon Storywriter (https://storywriter.amazon.com): Free
- Celtx (www.celtx.com): Free
- FadeIn (www.fadeinpro.com): One-time purchase
- Final Draft (https://store.finaldraft.com): One-time purchase; offers academic pricing
- Highland 2 (https://quoteunquoteapps.com/highland-2): Free or one-time purchase
- MovieMagic Screenwriter (www.screenplay.com): Offers academic pricing
- WriterDuet (www.writerduet.com): Free with optional upgrades

EDITING SOFTWARE

Impressively, the vast majority of all editing software, from the professional down to the entry level, is capable of the same functions. Inexpensive and free programs often have advanced features such as chroma key, titling, and audio/visual filters that would have been unavailable a decade ago. Which one to choose comes down to the ease of use of the interface and how easy and enjoyable the editing process is. Here is a brief rundown of some popular choices (please refer to the Glossary for terms you may not be familiar with):

EDITING SOFTWARE	COMPATIBILITY	PRICE	TYPE
Adobe Premier Pro - Considered the go-to for professional video editing, Premier is incredibly in-depth and works well with the rest of the Adobe family, including Photoshop and After Effects. There is a steep learning curve, and we don't usually recommend teaching it to students younger than high school age.	PC, Mac	$$$	Subscription
Final Cut Pro - Intuitive and powerful. Final Cut comes with many presets built in for easy effects and titles but does allow for fine-tuning. The background render function saves an incredible amount of time, something that has made it a popular choice for TV (particularly news and sports) where deadlines are important. This is our preferred software for working with children as they quickly grasp the basics and there are many audio and visual effect functions included for which most other platforms would require a third party app.	Mac	$$	One-time download
iMovie - For what a child is likely to produce, there is little that iMovie can't do that other professional software can. The titles, effects, and chroma key are all there, though it does limit the number of video and audio layers you can have. While the workflow is similar to Final Cut, iMovie's timeline is a little harder to work with. iMovie also works on iPads and iPhones which makes it a great option for schools that have those, although the touch-screen only editing can be frustrating.	Mac	Free	Available on any Apple product
WeVideo - A cloud-based editing software program, which frees up storage; this is especially useful if your computers are not particularly powerful. WeVideo also allows for collaboration outside the classroom. The editing process itself, however, is a bit clunky.	PC, Mac	Free	Paid Upgrades

SAFEGUARDS

How to distinguish between credible and non-credible sources: In order to guide students to credible resources on the web, we encourage teachers to preselect the resources they want students to use. In addition, teachers need to show students how to distinguish between credible and non-credible sources on the web and how to tell the difference between reliable facts, inaccurate or unsubstantiated facts, and opinion. One of the things you should drive home is the idea that video has the potential to reach a vastly larger audience than other media. If students are putting misinformation into their films, there could be a ripple effect; your student's audience is likely to be bigger, and for that reason, they need to get the facts straight.

Ask yourself: Are my students sourcing resources appropriately? Are they citing the same way they would with a five-paragraph essay or a creative writing assignment? In this case, the basic rules for citing sources in essays, reports, or films are the same. To do this simply put any citations at the end of the film in the credits. They don't need to be up for long; in fact your students can have them scroll quickly to save time.

Wikipedia is a great example of a resource that your students may want to use, but as you know it is not always the most credible. It's always good to have a couple different sources. Books—especially books where the author has cited multiple sources—are helpful. Whether you're pulling images off the web or out of books, make sure that you're leading your students to resources that are appropriate for their films.

When students are crediting other people or sources, the format depends on the scope of the audience. If it's internal, and you're just creating this video for your class, your students can write the bibliography and hand it in at the end of the assignment. If this is a project that's going on the web, however, students should cite the images and the music used throughout the film in the credits. Keep in mind that credit text can scroll quickly, but it should be there.

Protecting against cyber-bullying. Cyber-bullying is any type of online bullying. It happens predominantly on social media and YouTube, and it is an unfortunate reality. The best way to protect against cyber-bullying is to own your YouTube channel, monitor it closely, and delete videos and comments if needed. If necessary, you can turn the commenting feature off. You can also share videos privately, giving access only to those you choose. At Take Two we don't see any point in engaging with cyber-bullies and encourage you to quickly delete any negative comments. If it turns into a bigger issue, just delete the video. This is a learning program and about connecting video to the work that you are teaching in the classroom. As an educator, you have to decide where and how these conversations are going to happen in your classroom and beyond, and where, when, and how to set limits. Then you can adapt your policies as you learn; they don't have to be static.

Fair use and intellectual property. Your videos must not infringe on someone else's intellectual property. This is an important lesson for your students. Sourcing and referencing is required for all outside materials, images, video, or music that you or your students did not create. The principle is simple: anything you didn't create and record belongs to someone else and you can't use it without their explicit permission, or unless it falls under "fair use" usage guidelines. Fair use is the allowance of "brief excerpts of copyright material which

may, under certain circumstances, be quoted verbatim for purposes such as criticism, news reporting, teaching, and research, without the need for permission from or payment to the copyright holder."[14] You should let your students know that if there is any doubt on fair use, they need to use a substitute or seek permission. To qualify for fair use, your students' films should not be used to make money; they should be purely academic.

SUMMARY

- **Royalty-free Resources**
  - Have students look for B-roll, music, etc., that's royalty-free first.
- **Screenwriting Software and Editing Software**
  - You have a lot to choose from. Pick software that matches your budget and needs.
- **Safeguards**
  - Teach your students to differentiate between credible and noncredible sources.
  - Make sure your students cite their references appropriately.
  - Cyber-bullying: monitor and delete negative comments on online videos, or disable the commenting function.
  - Fair use: make sure that no one is monetizing your videos and have your students credit any component that was made by someone else.

---

14 Google Dictionary, 5/30/2019. For additional information on fair use standards, refer to the U.S. Copyright Office: https://www.copyright.gov/fair-use/more-info.html

PART 2

PRE-PRODUCTION

ARE YOU ACTIVELY ENGAGED OR IS IT A PASSIVE EXPERIENCE?

CHAPTER 5
VIEWING – THE NEW READING

When thinking about what to watch with your students, it's important to choose films that are good examples of what the students are about to make. This helps them immediately connect with the task at hand and to have a deeper understanding of what they are being asked to do. This chapter will look at passive versus active media consumption and how to engage your students in more active viewing experiences.

PASSIVE VERSUS ACTIVE MEDIA CONSUMPTION

An activity we like to do in the very beginning of a workshop with some of our older students (who have devices or phones that they use regularly) is to ask them to monitor their personal consumption of video and media for a week or so then share it with us in class. Most modern phones and devices allow you to see how much time you are spending looking at your screen. Apple devices, for instance, will track your social networking, productivity, reading, entertainment, creativity, and health and fitness.

We ask that the students bring a diary of their results to the class the following week and have an open conversation about how much of their time is spent in active or passive use of their devices. The main question is: who is doing the driving, you or the device? That is, are you actively engaged or is it a passive experience? It's important to get students to start to bring this idea of active viewing into the films you watch with them.

ENCOURAGE ACTIVE VIEWING

Media literacy is the ability to dissect and analyze the content we watch. In the same way that we teach students to analyze what they read, we need to teach them the grammar associated with what they watch. Viewing a film or piece of media can easily become a passive activity; it's important to model an active viewing experience for your students so they can bring that same intention to the films they make.

Pro Tip! A note catcher is a great tool to have handy whenever you are watching something with your students. It encourages them into an active viewing position and helps them engage with what you are showing them.

How should you watch something with your students? Draw their attention to what it is they are seeing and what it is they are hearing (the third dimension). Try watching a short film (under five minutes long) in its entirety, either Documentary or Narrative film, without any prompts or context. Then watch it again, this time with the note catcher, and ask the students:

- **Is this a Documentary or Narrative film?**
    - How do you decide?
    - What's the difference?

- **If it's a Documentary film:**
    - What is the genre, e.g., historical, investigative, personal, informational, or propagandist?

- What do you hear? How does music affect the feeling of the film?
- What do you see? How do the images shape or augment the message of the film?
- What B-roll is being used (archival, production footage, images)? To what effect?
- If there is an interview, how and where was it filmed? In what way does it add to the credibility of the film?
- Do you feel the film is credible? Why or why not?
- What was the filmmaker's main goal or message? How well did they achieve it?

- **If it's a Narrative film:**

  - What is the story arc?
  - Answer the Five W questions.
  - What is the genre, e.g., science fiction, mystery, drama?
  - What kind of shots do you see and how many cuts were there (wide, medium, close up, extreme close up)? (See Chapter 8 and the Glossary for more on these terms.)
  - Where was the camera (e.g., on a track, tripod, dolly, drone, or crane)? How did this impact the feeling of the film?
  - What music or sound effects did you hear? How did sound impact the feeling of the film?
  - What was the main purpose or message of the film? How well did the filmmaker convey it?

Through these conversations you will be able to pull apart and understand the true intentions of the director and writers, just as you do when dissecting and analyzing a piece of written material.

Remember, for all age levels, you need to find films that are short (no more than five - ten minutes) and appropriate for the grade level. You can also find some great film choices on our community board on our LMS.

CHAPTER 6
DOCUMENTARY FILM: THE NEW ESSAY

In this chapter we will outline the pre-production steps required to produce a Documentary film with your class, and provide samples of a rubric, production calendar, and script. The steps you'll be following are:

1. Select Your Topic
2. Choose the Documentary Type
3. Create Rubric
4. Introduce Topic and Rubric
5. Watch an Example
6. Hold a Brainstorming Session
7. Conduct Research
8. Write the Script

SELECT YOUR TOPIC

Choose a topic that enables students to feel a real sense of agency around what they're going to learn. You want to ignite their curiosity. As an educator, you want to pick a topic that you think your students are going to get excited about, what they gravitate towards. At the end of the day, your students are the ones making the film, and they're the ones who are going to be teaching the other students in their class.

It's helpful if the topic is a bit broad, but not so wide open that it's difficult for students to narrow the topic according to their own interest. In a history class, perhaps students can investigate the different factors (politics, economy, climate, culture, and technology) of an ancient society they are studying. In a science class, students could choose between different environmental threats and how to address them. In an English class, students can create historical biographies based on authors they are studying. The topic should be wide enough that the students feel they can make the film their own, but not so wide that they might drown in the possibilities.

CHOOSE THE TYPE OF DOCUMENTARY

Documentaries, like Narrative films, have their own genres and approaches to the subject matter. There are four core types of Documentary film: historical, informative, investigatory, and personal. A fifth category, propaganda, shares production similarities with the others though it's important to recognize the material difference in the approach it takes to presenting facts.

For historical documentary, think PBS or Ken Burns. Here, you're researching and understanding a historical topic by collecting archival footage, interviewing experts in that area or in that subject matter, and shooting on location. For example, maybe you're shooting in a historical landmark and you're going to interview someone on site who really knows about that historic location. A historical documentary presents information in a simple, unbiased manner, with the filmmaker's own thoughts on the matter left outside of the film. A historical documentary might be looked at like a video book report, with your student filmmakers presenting what they've studied in class in a thorough and fair way.

Investigatory documentary is used when you're investigating an idea or a topic to create discussion. A good example of this is the 2016 documentary

Before the Flood, starring Leonardo DiCaprio. In the film, DiCaprio meets with scientists, activists, and world leaders to "discuss the dangers of climate change and possible solutions." This results in a really wonderful example of what investigatory film can do. The film feels somewhat personal, because DiCaprio is walking around talking to all these experts, but what he's really doing is investigating a subject.

This is similar to Michael Moore's films, which also feel personal, because Moore is such a prominent character in his documentaries. The audience is getting a very high-level investigatory approach. Although the film does include a lot of facts, it usually presents a very one-sided perspective. A lot of experts are cherry-picked to tell the story that the documentarian wants to tell, while investigating a specific idea and a specific topic, which has more complexity.

In an investigatory documentary, the investigation is the star, but the filmmaker's personal stake in the project is often at the forefront. This style suits a subject matter that does not have a clear outcome, giving your students scope to pose an essential question to the audience, such as: "Is climate change affecting our way of life?" or "How did this historical event change the course of history?"

Personal documentary is where the protagonist embarks on a journey of discovery. It could be self-discovery. It could be discovering a personal matter of the hero's past or of his or her family, and it's usually very dramatic. An example would be Sarah Polley's 2012 film *Stories We Tell*. The film takes a look at the relationship between Polley's parents while exploring how her perception of their marriage shaped her as an individual. It includes interviews, home video footage, and reenactments. One way to look at the "personal documentary" style is as a video autobiography.

Informational documentary is just purely instructive. It tends not to be so investigatory, and is more like a public service announcement (PSA), explicitly stating, "Here's the information you need to know." It could be thought of as a marketing video where you're communicating the information an audience needs to know directly.

On the whole, when it comes to making Documentaries (no matter the type), educators should think of the project as a way of turning the typical research paper, investigatory idea, or personal essay into a film.

Propaganda films can be a fun way to explore two or more sides of an argument. It's important for students to understand what propaganda means. We like to show child-friendly examples to make the points. Propaganda is a one-sided opinion piece that doesn't necessarily use all the facts. It can use fear, satire, or self-aggrandization to persuade viewers into a particular opinion. Propaganda films are constructed in much the same way as a documentary, but they do allow students greater creativity in coming up with their own B-roll.

INTRODUCE TOPIC AND RUBRIC

Once you've discussed which unit of study your students will be researching for their documentaries, introduce the rubric for how they will be assessed. You want to have some benchmarks for what you want your students to learn from a filmmaking point of view, but you also want traditional benchmarks for what you want your students to learn specifically about the subject. You drive the content. The filmmaking and media comprehension piece is just the literacy vehicle that allows your students to communicate what they are learning.

The rubric should include benchmarks for understanding the technical components of making a film, but also for whatever content outcomes you want to establish for your students. Our rubrics include questions like: Was there a solid beginning, middle, and end? Was the story told effectively? How were the images used? And then there are assessment questions such as: Was this well done, medium, or satisfactory?

We have different rubrics for Narrative and Documentary films. Narrative has a little more creative spin: How was the acting? Were there interesting shots used? How did the music play into the film? For Documentary, the rubric needs

to evaluate how successfully the filmmakers relay their information or subject matter to the audience. Was the audience left with some new knowledge of the topic? Did they come to understand the issues better? Were the facts correct?

You want to make sure that you're creating a rubric specific for the project at hand. You want to bring in some elements of filmmaking for the students to learn, but you also want to assess their analytical competencies: *Are they understanding and conveying the information well?*

One way you can make the rubric part of the overall process is to hand it out to your audience. In filmmaking, it is ultimately the audience's experience that we are trying to shape. During your screening, it's fun to have the audience fill out the rubric. This way, you can have an assessment done—all conducted by the students watching one another's films—asking questions like: "Did you get it? Are these films communicating what we need to have communicated? How was the story? Was it good? Was there a good solid beginning, middle, and end? Was there an effective call to action? Do we all understand the issues better?"

To the right is an example of one of our rubrics to measure achievement in the area of filmmaking and media comprehension. We recommend sharing a document like this with the filmmaking teams who can then use this document to do their research and pre-production.

You can also use this QR code[15] to link to our Learning Manage-ment System for more examples that show how to assess the content so it aligns with your schools standards or the Common Core.

15 Learning Management System.

SAMPLE RUBRIC FOR FILM LITERACY

LEARNING TARGET	4- EXEMPLARY	3- PROFICIENT	2- APPRENTICE	1- BEGINNER
Integrity/ Communication I can be honest and respectful in my daily interactions.	I can respectfully collaborate and communicate with my peers in a way that improves our classroom culture.	I can respectfully collaborate and communicate with my peers.	I sometimes struggle to collaborate and communicate with my peers.	I struggle to communicate and work collaboratively with my peers.
I can understand and analyze film and media.	I can watch a documentary and highly understand what the director's intentions are and how the film was made, and analyze my own thoughts and reactions to the film.	I can watch a documentary and understand what the director's intentions are and how the film was made, and analyze my own thoughts and reactions to the film.	I can watch a documentary and somewhat understand what the director's intentions are and how the film was made, and analyze my own thoughts and reactions to the film.	I can't watch a documentary and understand what the director's intentions are and how the film was made, and analyze my own thoughts and reactions to the film.
I can create an effective and thought-provoking film that will incite change.	I can research, write, and create an exemplary film that is very well edited and shows the past, present, and future of a problem and has a compelling call to action.	I can research, write, and create a good film that is edited and shows the past, present, and future of a problem and has a compelling call to action.	I can research, write, and create a film that is edited and shows a few parts of either the past, present, or future of a problem and has a call to action.	I cannot research, write, and create a film that is edited well and that has examples of the past, present, and future of a problem as well as a call to action.

Total Score: _____

SAMPLE PRODUCTION CALENDAR

CALENDAR						
SUNDAY	**MONDAY**	**TUESDAY**	**WEDNESDAY**	**THURSDAY**	**FRIDAY**	**SATURDAY**
	This week would be good to introduce the students to the project and give them some background knowledge.					
	4/8 Intro/ screening series (analysis)	4/9 Screening series (analysis)	4/10 Start to write script in groups	4/11 Write script	4/12 Write script	
	4/15 Record VO	4/16 Record VO	4/17 Start to edit	4/18 Edit	4/19 Edit	
	4/22 Screening					

Here is an example of how we would present the calendar to the class.

WATCH AN EXAMPLE

See Chapter 5 for more on how to do this, but you want to analyze any film you watch with your students for story, sound design, editing, direction, and how well it conveys knowledge and advocacy for a cause. You can use a note catcher for questions such as:

- What did you think of the editing, the B-roll, story, and sound design?

- What made this film good? Where could it be improved? What were the strengths? What were the weaknesses?

- Was there a solid beginning, middle, and end?

- What were you listening to? What were you hearing during the film? Did you hear the music? What did the music do? Did the music make you feel something, or was the music ineffective? Where do you think they got the music from? Is the music original? Did they find it from online sources? Is it royalty-free?

- Did you hear a voice-over or see text cards? Did the images work well with the audio and text? What images were being used? If you heard a voice-over and you saw images, were the images compatible with what you were hearing?

- Did you notice how a still image was moving in or moving out? Do you know why that's called the Ken Burns effect?

- Where did they find the images? Does it look like someone went and shot them specifically for this film? Who owns the image when someone shoots their own film?

You want to pull the curtain back and deconstruct the film. As you pose these questions, you're creating a "to-do" list for each student's project, and down the road you can refer to the example film to remind them of what constitutes a successful film. "Remember how music was used in so-and-so?" "Would text cards highlighting facts and figures work here like they did in the other film?"

As you build your film program, you can start to use documentaries made from previous classes. That's particularly fun because then students can actually see, "Oh, this is where the previous class left off. I see what's expected of me and where I need to go."

HOLD A BRAINSTORMING SESSION

After watching some films, and assuming that you haven't already assigned the groups and projects, you can hold a brainstorming session with the students. Give them ten minutes to brainstorm on their own and then share their ideas with the group. Be sure everyone has the chance to speak and to be heard. Encourage all students to share their ideas. Once all ideas are on the board do a silent, anonymous vote to determine which films to make that session. Arrange students in groups of three to five depending on who works well together and which film they are interested in.

This brainstorming session can work in two ways: one, have students share elements about the subject that they already know; or two, have them pitch ideas for films.

For example, say you are going to make Documentary films about Native Americans. Using the first method, you might ask your students what they know about Native Americans. You might get responses like: "I know they hunted and gathered their own food. They made tools out of any and all materials they could find. They lived in tribes and their families extended past a mother, father, child." By sharing their knowledge, students are developing research topics based on what they already know.

The second method for a brainstorming session is preferable if your class is a little more advanced. By pitching ideas, they help solidify other students' interests, and groups can be formed based on that. Encourage your students to pitch their ideas in rapid fire, but everyone just says one idea in turn. Using the same documentary example, they might say: "I want to make a film that explores how the Native Americans made their tools. I want to make a historical documentary about the spiritual practices of the Mohawk Tribe."

You might go through three or more rounds to get all the ideas. Once you have all the ideas up on the board, hold a blind, silent voting session where everyone puts his or her head down, and then raises their hand for the ideas that they like. We strongly encourage anonymous voting because that way students are voting based on their genuine interests, not voting on the topics their friends vote for, or even worse, not voting for a topic because their friends did not vote. Once you have a manageable set of ideas, assign student groups to the selected projects. The students then get to be a part of a group that is making a film about something they care about, again promoting agency.

These are your students: you know who works well together, and what they're capable of doing. If you want to choose the groups and the topics, that's completely up to you. This is just a strategy we've used to help students have higher levels of engagement and agency in what they create. Remember that group size is critical: if you have six or more students in a group, then you will likely have two or three who are just not engaged because they're not doing anything. For Documentary, we have found that three to five students per group is ideal.

CONDUCT RESEARCH

Let your students manage a lot of the project on their own, but continue to encourage them to delve deeper into the investigation and gather more evidence or information. Here, you are going to provide tips and tools for researching a topic. Depending on the grade level, students may already have strong tools for conducting research; use the method that works best for your teaching style. As long as the students use their research skills to create a strong beginning, middle, and end with a concluding call to action, they will be in good shape.

Once your students have formed into groups, they'll start working on a Google Doc (see below for an example on how to organize the script) so they can share information. You will also be showing them how to do research within the Google Doc.

It's important that you prepare some credible sites, books, or other sources ahead of time to make sure that students are collecting the correct facts. To do this, we recommend having links to online resources in the Google Doc so that students can visit them directly, or, if you have books that you recommend, you can make them available in your classroom or at the school library. That way, students can go through the books and do research. You'll be guiding your students in their research, and since every class will have different levels of literacy and research skills you will need to work with the needs of each class.

If your students are doing an investigatory, current events-oriented, or social action film, you want to make sure that they have a good call to action at the end. Audience members should be left thinking, "Oh, I can take shorter showers" or "I can donate to this nonprofit," and so on.

Stress to your students that part of their job as filmmakers is to only include valid and confirmed research or information in their films. They have a responsibility to provide their audience with the truth. This is part of the unspoken agreement between a filmmaker and the audience: I promise to provide you with factual information so you can make your own informed opinion; if our opinions happen to align, or I've caused you to think about your perspective, then I've successfully done my job.

16 Video of Documentary.

WRITE THE SCRIPT

It's important that the unit of study you use for Documentary film is aligned with a strong claim or thesis and can have an interesting call to action or leave the audience with a compelling conclusion. You still want to emphasize that the films should have a strong BME, and should be based on a robust outline. Think of a documentary as a five paragraph essay for the Digital Age. Start with an introduction, and aim for three "supporting paragraphs" that each reinforce a key proof point. Encourage your students to limit each "paragraph" to a few sentences with no redundancies. For example: the first of the three supporting paragraphs can be about the subject's past, the second about its present-day status, and the third about its probable future. End with a conclusion that contains a call to action encouraging the audience to continue their participation in your subject matter after the screening. It can be as simple as asking the audience to do their own research or investigation afterwards, or it can be as big as asking them to "sign this petition," "call this Congressman," or "donate your time or resources to this foundation."

Remember that in film, if you say the same thing twice your audience will lose interest. Keep introducing new ideas and facts!

A documentary screenplay is typically divided into two columns. The left column is an Audio column. It consists of voice-over (VO) writing, sample questions for interviews, and ideas for the overall soundscape of the film. The right column is the video column. It includes ideas for primary footage (often times an interview), B-roll (or secondary footage used to bolster your VO), archival footage, graphs, charts, animations, and more visuals that should connect directly to what your audience hears.

SAMPLE DOCUMENTARY SCRIPT

AUDIO	VIDEO - B-ROLL: FOUND FOOTAGE AND ARCHIVAL IMAGE
Intro: What is the environmental problem you are concerned about? Ex.: *Today we are seeing a lot of marine debris in our oceans.*	
Body Paragraph 1 (past): How did this problem come to be?	
Body Paragraph 2 (present): What is going on now?	
Body Paragraph 3 (future): What will happen if nothing is done?	
Conclusion (call to action): What can we do to stop it?	

Pro Tip! Assign each student a paragraph, but have them collaborate on what should be in each paragraph. What's good about Google Docs is that the members of the groups can read what others have written. Encourage your students to limit each paragraph to a few sentences per paragraph so that their films are manageable and won't take a month to create!

SUMMARY

- **Select your topic**
    - What part of your curriculum will lend itself well to experimenting with film?
- **Choose the type of Documentary you want to make with your students**
    - Historical, Investigative, Informational, Personal, or Propaganda.
- **Create rubric**
    - Your rubric should have assessments for both the third dimension of literacy and the content of the study.
- **Introduce topic and rubric**
- **Watch an example**
    - Show examples to give your students a goal to reach for.

- **Hold a brainstorming session**

- **Conduct research**
    - Conducting research should be designed for the level of your class. You may need to give your students specific books or print-outs, or you can let them be more autonomous; just make sure the facts they find are correct.

- **Write the script**
    - Have the groups divide up the tasks of writing each section of the film. This will allow them to work quickly and check each other's work.

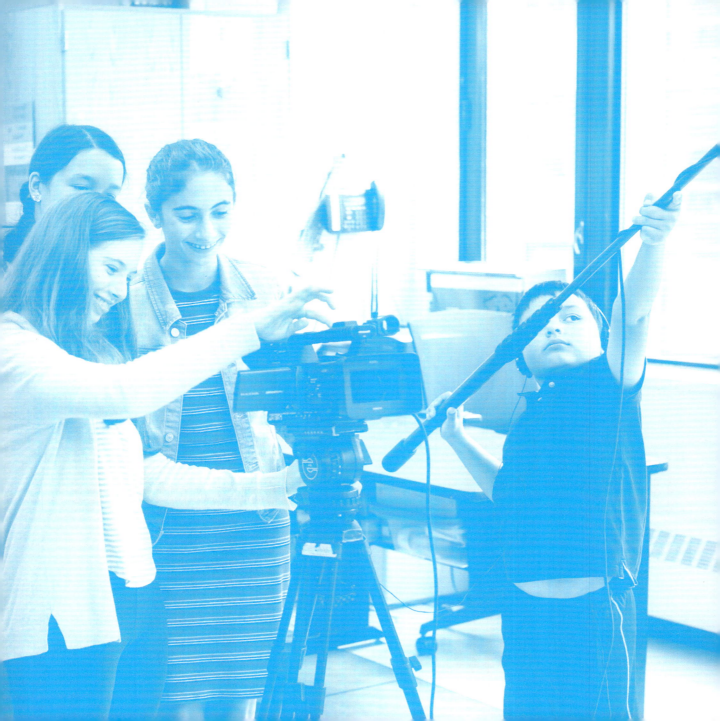

CHAPTER 7
NARRATIVE AND SILENT FILMS: THE NEW CREATIVE WRITING ASSIGNMENT

If Documentary filmmaking is the new essay for the digital age then Narrative filmmaking is the new creative writing. Now that you've familiarized yourself with the resources you'll need to help your students produce a great film, you're ready to enter the pre-production phase of a Narrative or Silent film. In this chapter, we will run through the various steps necessary to create great Narrative films with your students, whether they be silent or full of dialogue.

We'll be going over techniques and process for use with live action rather than animation. If you would like to do animation projects please visit our LMS for how-tos and lesson plans. One upside to animations is that you record audio separately, similar to documentaries, which reduces the risk of external noise disruptions.

Pro Tip! Making short silent films with your students can be a great introduction to Narrative film and allows you to teach a lot about story structure, shots, and editing without having to worry about capturing clean audio.

Here are the pre-production steps you'll be following:

1. Introduce Topic and Rubric
2. Teach Story Structure
3. Watch Examples and Choose a Genre
4. Hold a Brainstorming Session
5. Develop Plot Treatment
6. Write the Screenplay
7. Storyboard the Film

17 LMS templates and rubrics.

INTRODUCE TOPIC AND RUBRIC

Pick the unit of study you want your students to make their Narrative or Silent films about, and introduce the rubric for how they will be assessed. We use the following type of rubric in the beginning as it outlines both expectations and timeline. You should also add an assessment line for the content you want them to have learned.

You can also use this QR code[17] to find other templates and rubrics on our LMS for inspiration.

SAMPLE NARRATIVE FILM RUBRIC

LEARNING TARGET	4- EXEMPLARY	3- PROFICIENT	2- APPRENTICE	1- BEGINNER
Integrity/ Communication I can be honest and respectful in my daily interactions.	I can respectfully collaborate and communicate with my peers in a way that improves our classroom culture.	I can respectfully collaborate and communicate with my peers.	I sometimes struggle to collaborate and communicate with my peers.	I struggle to communicate and work collaboratively with my peers.
I can convey elements of the topic through the narrative structure of a Hero's Journey.	Within my analysis of the elements, I include evidence from class and analyze how it connects to that element.	I have correctly applied 5 elements of the film topic and analyzed how it was used in my film.	I have correctly applied at least 4 elements of the film topic and analyzed how it was used in my film.	I have correctly applied 3 or fewer elements of the film topic and analyzed how it was used in my film.
I can understand and analyze film and media.	I can watch a narrative film and highly understand what the director's intentions are, how the film was made, and analyze my own thoughts and reactions to the film.	I can watch a narrative film and understand what the director's intentions are, how the film was made, and analyze my own thoughts and reactions to the film.	I can watch a narrative film and somewhat understand what the director's intentions are, how the film was made, and analyze my own thoughts and reactions to the film.	I can't watch a narrative film and understand what the director's intentions are, how the film was made, and analyze my own thoughts and reactions to the film.
I can create an entertaining and thought-provoking film.	I can write, and create an exemplary film that is very well edited and shows elements of the hero's journey.	I can write, and create a good film that is edited and shows elements of the hero's journey.	I can write, and create a film that is edited and shows a few elements of the hero's journey.	I cannot write, and create a film that is edited well and includes elements of the hero's journey.

Total Score: _____

SAMPLE NARRATIVE PRODUCTION CALENDAR

CALENDAR						
SUNDAY	**MONDAY**	**TUESDAY**	**WEDNESDAY**	**THURSDAY**	**FRIDAY**	**SATURDAY**
	This week would be a good time to introduce the students to the project and give them some background knowledge.					
	4/8 Intro/ screening series (analysis)	4/9 Screening series (analysis)	4/10 Brainstorm /Outine	4/11 Write script	4/12 Write script	
	4/15 Location Scout/ Story board	4/16 Shoot	4/17 Shoot	4/18 Shoot	4/19 Shoot	
	4/22 Edit	4/23 Edit	4/24 Edit	4/25 Edit	4/26 Screening	

TEACH STORY STRUCTURE

Consider narrative filmmaking a creative writing assignment. Have students outline the traditional story arc and answer the Five W questions: *who* are the protagonist, antagonist, foil, and mentor; *what* are the obstacles the antagonist creates for the protagonist; *where* and *when* does the story take place (challenge your students to create ways to show their setting, rather than just telling the audience); and *why* is this a story worth telling? Also, identify the plot, featuring a clear BME.

A great way to start is to lead a discussion on what makes a great story and by extension, what makes a great film. Now is the ideal time to introduce your students to the concept of the **Hero's Journey**.

The modern notion of the Hero's Journey derives from Joseph Campbell's *The Hero with a Thousand Faces*,[18] in which the author posited that all storytelling follows a certain pattern, which he calls the "monomyth." He explains it as such:

A hero ventures forth from the world of common day into a region of supernatural wonder (x): fabulous forces are there encountered and a decisive victory is won (y): the hero comes back from this mysterious adventure with the power to bestow boons on his fellow man (z).[19]

---

[18] Christopher Vogler, The Writer's Journey, 3rd Edition, Michael Wiese Productions, 2007, p. 4.
[19] Joseph Campbell, The Hero with A Thousand Faces,.New World Library, 2008, p. 23.

In *The Writer's Journey*, Christopher Vogler adapts Campbell's vision into twelve stages:

Stage 1: Ordinary World
Stage 2: Call to Adventure
Stage 3: Refusal of the Call
Stage 4: Meeting with the Mentor
Stage 5: Crossing the First Threshold
Stage 6: Tests, Allies, Enemies
Stage 7: Approach to the Inmost Cave
Stage 8: Ordeal
Stage 9: Reward (Seizing the Sword)
Stage 10: The Road Back
Stage 11: Resurrection
Stage 12: Return with the Elixir[20]

"At heart," writes Vogler, "the hero's story is always a journey. A hero leaves her comfortable, ordinary surroundings to venture into a challenging, unfamiliar world. It may be an outward journey to an actual place." On the other hand, he explains, "…there are as many stories that take the hero on an inward journey, one of the mind, the heart, the spirit. In any good story the hero grows and changes…It's these emotional journeys that hook an audience and make a story worth watching."[21]

As you talk with your students about the ingredients of effective storytelling, it's impactful to show them a journey. Outline the story arc, go over the Five Ws, then show or cite some films that demonstrate these concepts well (see Chapter 5 for ideas on how to do this effectively).

---

20 Vogler., p. 8.
21 Vogler, p. 7.

WATCH EXAMPLES AND CHOOSE A GENRE

Show your students that story structure can be used in any and all genres. Create a running list of genres that your students are already aware of and introduce them to new ones. You may have a genre in mind that you want the class to focus on, e.g., Coming of Age (great for high school English), Post-Apocalyptic Dystopian (great for issued-based or science focuses like climate change, extinction, technology), or Historical Fiction (great for social studies). You can also let your students select a genre and give them a topic to focus on, like bullying, community building, homelessness, the environment, or disease. The topics and genres are endless!

To give your students a visual example of the work they're about to do, visit the Take Two YouTube Channel[22] and watch a few films from different genres. They'll see the story structure at work and get an idea of what their finished product should look like.

22 Take Two YouTube Channel.

HOLD A BRAINSTORMING SESSION

Now you are ready to begin a brainstorming exercise[23] with your class. When it comes to student-produced films, great narratives are birthed from great brainstorming sessions. These sessions are delicate endeavors. You'll want to guide your students while still allowing them to plant their own creative seeds—the seeds from which their own unique voice will grow and prosper. At the same time you want to be vigilant that students respect one another; they need to feel safe to share and suggest their own ideas and vision. It is important to continue to remind your students that every single idea is a good idea.

23 Video of Brainstorm Session.

1. Give students 10 minutes to brainstorm on their own. Encourage students to do this independently by quietly writing down or drawing their ideas. They will be collaborating with their friends on every other aspect of this project, and this is their one opportunity to explore all the avenues of their creativity without having to compromise. It's wonderful if you have students who are able to come up with multiple ideas complete with characters and full story arcs, but this is unlikely to happen for everyone and that's okay. At Take Two, we encourage students to put down any idea no matter how big or small. Maybe they can only think of the beginning to their movie, maybe they only have an idea for a character but can't figure out what's going to happen to them, or maybe all they have is an interesting title or genre they are excited about. All of this is something that can be used by their peers to create a compelling project.

Complete creative freedom can often be a little daunting. If your students find themselves unable to narrow down their creativity, you might want to encourage them to select a common theme. We once worked with students who were asked to make movies that connected to the theme of "Me to We": their protagonists needed to begin their film as an individual and find some kind of community by the end. At another school we worked with students who were tasked to include elements of P.B.I.S. (Positive Behavior Intervention and Support). Having a unifying theme in the class project doesn't limit the creativity, but instead offers a North Star to guide them (and it helps by providing their narratives from the beginning with a little more substance than just some adolescent humor or action sequences).

2. Have students share their ideas with the group. Go around the room and have each student share one idea at a time in a short "elevator pitch." Students who have more than one idea will share their second or third ideas on the next pass. Again make sure that everyone has a chance to speak and be heard. Let that one shy student in the back know her idea could be the idea that inspires the entire class to make the best movie possible. We typically encourage students to share these ideas one at a time and not as an open forum. If a student has a question or is inspired with a new idea, they should write it down and share it during their next turn.

3. Write all ideas on a whiteboard/blackboard/easel.

4. Hold an anonymous vote to determine which films to make this session. Have the students close their eyes and vote for as many ideas as they like. We encourage students to vote anonymously so they're choosing the idea they're actually excited about, not just voting for the ones their friends like. (Or worse, not voting because their friends didn't.) Continue to do this until you come up with enough ideas to make groups of three to six students. Try to form the groups based on interest but make sure you think any chosen idea will ultimately be workable. Assure students that even if their idea isn't the main subject of their film, they'll find exciting ways to incorporate other ideas.

DEVELOP PLOT TREATMENT

24 Video of Story.

Once you have all groups arranged, your students are ready to start writing a plot treatment. A *treatment* is the backbone of what will eventually become your students' screenplay. It covers the story arc and structure in a format that is more detailed than an outline, but less developed than the script itself.

Each team should be given a large sheet of paper and some pens where they can write out a draft treatment that will include a story arc and structure. Students should be instructed to ask and answer the Five Ws.

- *Who* is the protagonist? Does the protagonist have to be a "good guy"?
- *Who* is the antagonist? Does the antagonist have to be a "bad guy"? Does the antagonist even have to be human? For example maybe the antagonist is the weather or a meteor (man versus environment), or society (man versus society)?
- *Who* is the foil (sidekick) or mentor? How do their skills differ from those of the protagonist? How do their skills benefit the protagonist?
- *When* does this story take place?
- *Where* is this story set? In filmmaking, it's important that you show your audience the setting, rather than just use a title card (for instance, a shot of the New York City skyline rather than a title card that says "New York City, 2018").
- *Where* do you plan to film your movie? (Take Two strongly

recommends that adults supervise all off-campus filming.)

- *What* is the call to adventure/the key challenge or question that sets up the narrative arc?
- *What* are the obstacles and challenges that the protagonist will face? In filmmaking, the first obstacle is often called the "inciting incident."
- How can this be folded into a BME?
- How will characters change over time?
- *Why* is this story worth telling? Why should the audience care?

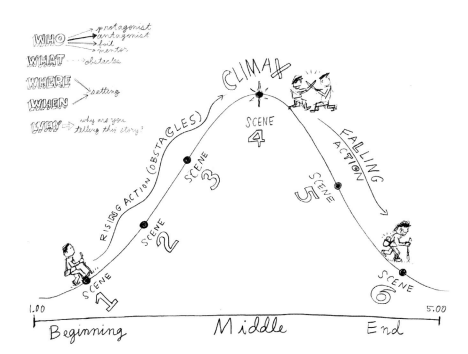

WRITE THE SCREENPLAY

A good plot treatment will set the table for a great screenplay. Take Two recommends using a cloud-based writing tool so that students can collaborate in real time. We have put templates for Google Docs and Microsoft Word/OneNote online. If you'd prefer to create your own template or format your students' work, the basic components of a screenplay are below.

Guide to the screenplay format: Traditionally, screenplays begin with a cover page with the title of the film in all capital letters, centered, in size 12 Courier font. On the next line are the names of the screenwriters, centered, in title case.

The body pages are also in font size 12. Traditionally the margins are as follows:

- Top margin = 1 inch
- Left margin = 1.5 inches
- Right margin = 1.25 inches
- Bottom margin = 1 inch

25 Video Screewriting.

26 Sample Screen Play.

The top page has a page number followed by a period in the upper right hand corner. Character names are in all caps and indented 3.7 inches. Before writing any dialogue, there should be a scene number and header (the location of the scene) and an action which describes everything you will see on the screen.

You can download a complete sample screenplay from Take Two's LMS.[26]

Alternatively, there are many good screenwriting software packages that will take care of formatting for you and your students. Much like editing software, each has different features and advantages. Final Draft is the industry standard and intuitively formats the text as you write, but it's very expensive and does not offer updates after purchase. Celtx and Amazon Storyteller are free

Capitalize location.
INT = interior,
EXT = Exterior

Capitalize the first time you meet a character.

Capitalize sound effect.

Capitalize prop.

Parentheses emotion.

Capitalize small, important details.

Underline and capitalize the title.

<u>My Very First Movie</u>

Written by
Megan Kiefer

Scene 1
INT. LIBRARY
MEGAN, 13, tiptoes into the library. Only a few lights are on, and it's surprisingly empty. She looks around hoping to find a familiar face.

          MEGAN
    Hello? Is anyone here?

Megan jumps at the sound of an ENTIRE BOOKCASE FALLING behind her. She whips around and sees JASON, 12, standing before the fallen bookcase.

          JASON
    Whoops.

Megan GRUMBLES as she walks up to her friend.

          MEGAN
    Look what you did! We're going to get in a lot of trouble.

          JASON
    Nevermind that! Look what I found...

Jason reveals to Megan and OLD DUSTY BOOK titled "Magic Spells for a Rainy Day."

          MEGAN
      (skeptical)
    That's not real.

          JASON
    Yes huh! And I found just the spell for us to try.

Jason FLIPS THROUGH the pages and shows Megan his spell of choice: "How to Make Your Dog Fly." Megan lights up, suddenly a belier.

          MEGAN
    Let's take this home right now!

Scene 2
EXT. Megan's Backyard
    Megan and ason stand before her best corgi RUFUS.

          MEGAN
    Alright Rufus, stay.

Megan opens the book to the spell.

          MEGAN
    From the ground and to the sky, pick up this dog and make him fly!

Example of the screenplay format.

and great for beginners, but more seasoned and quick-moving writers might become frustrated with their limitations. And it never hurts to start off simple with Google Docs. Being in control of your own formatting allows a writer to truly understand why the format is necessary and how it aids production. Ask your students what they think their project needs, and then you can select the software that suits them best.

One of the most difficult but important parts of the screenplay drafting process is writing dialogue. To help your students write the best lines of dialogue, remind them that they are not constrained by writing in complete sentences. Students may want to quietly say the lines out loud as they write them, or act out the scene as they listen to hear how it sounds. And generally a good script turns into a great one after a table read: let students read their scripts to their classmates, with the appropriate performers reading for each part. This does two things: it lets the writers witness how an audience reacts to their story, the good and the bad; and it helps bring some reality to the project. This is a real movie, and an audience may laugh or cry or get chills from what they do. It's an exciting, empowering experience. Remind your students to provide feedback respectfully to one another during a table read. Their classmates are being vulnerable and sharing their work. That's worth applauding.

STORYBOARD THE FILM

Before we storyboard, we tell our students it's time to take off their writers' hats and put on their directors' hats. Storyboarding is planning and drawing out the shots you are going to use before you actually start to shoot. What you want to teach at this stage is how to plan the best shots for the story. (For a complete guide to the types of shots, camera angles, and equipment, refer to Chapter 8.)

27 Video of Storyboarding, Actors and Locations.

We then ask our students to divide the script up so each student is in charge of a specific scene to storyboard. Then they start to draw how they are going to shoot the scene. Using rudimentary drawing such as stick figures is fine. They can use the below template to circle their answers so you can see what they are thinking (sometimes it's hard to discern their ideas from their drawings). For instance, is this shot a Master or Coverage (this means is the shot capturing the entire scene or just a piece of it?) Is it a wide, medium, close-up, extreme close-up? Where will the camera be and what will it be doing? Will it be low, high, bird's-eye view, on a dolly or crane, zooming in or out? (These techniques are covered in more detail in Chapter 8). These are all questions your students should be thinking about now. You may not have access to equipment that would enable every option, but it's still good to get your students to start thinking like directors.

Story Boards

Movie _____
Scene # _____

Circle your answer:
Shot: Master, Coverage
Extreme Close Up, Close Up, Medium, Wide
Camera Position:
Low, Center, High, Bird's Eye, POV (Point of View), Dolly, Rack, Pan, Tilt, Zoom in, out
Characters/Focus of Shot:

Circle your answer:
Shot: Master, Coverage
Extreme Close Up, Close Up, Medium, Wide
Camera Position:
Low, Center, High, Bird's Eye, POV (Point of View), Dolly, Rack, Pan, Tilt, Zoom in, out
Characters/Focus of Shot:

Circle your answer:
Shot: Master, Coverage
Extreme Close Up, Close Up, Medium, Wide
Camera Position:
Low, Center, High, Bird's Eye, POV (Point of View), Dolly, Rack, Pan, Tilt, Zoom in, out
Characters/Focus of Shot:

Circle your answer:
Shot: Master, Coverage
Extreme Close Up, Close Up, Medium, Wide
Camera Position:
Low, Center, High, Bird's Eye, POV (Point of View), Dolly, Rack, Pan, Tilt, Zoom in, out
Characters/Focus of Shot:

Storyboard Template Example.

SUMMARY

- **Introduce Topic and Rubric**
  - Create a rubric that has assessment for both the filmmaking component and for the content. Introduce the schedule.

- **Teach Story Structure**
  - Go over the Five Ws and the Hero's Journey.

- **Watch Examples and Choose a Genre**
  - Find films that correlate to the films your students will make. Ask them questions and engage them in active watching.

- **Hold a Brainstorming Session**
  - Give students 10 minutes to brainstorm on their own.
  - Have students share their ideas with the group. Write all ideas where the whole class can see (on a whiteboard, blackboard, easel, etc.).
  - Hold an anonymous vote to determine which films to make this session.

- **Develop Plot Treatment**
  - Have students answer the Five Ws and create the BME.
- **Write the Screenplay**
  - Teach screenplay formatting and have students collaborate on writing the script.
- **Storyboard the Film**
  - Teach students how to pick shots and how to plan for the production days (reference Chapter 8 for more detail.

PART 3:
PRODUCTION

CHAPTER 8
THE GRAMMAR OF FILMMAKING

Getting the shot for both Documentary or Narrative film allows your students to speak the grammar of filmmaking! In order for your students to communicate in this medium effectively they need to become familiar with the different types of camera shots, all of which can convey particular meaning or set a unique tone. This chapter will outline all the typical camera shots and why they are used.

CAMERA SHOTS

We teach students that there are four main shots: Wide, Medium, Close-up, and Extreme Close-up. They each have uses and suggest certain things to the audience.

A *Wide Shot* shows your subject's entire body plus the space they're in. Sometimes it's called the *Establishing Shot* as it gives your audience a lot of useful information: who is in the scene, where are they, and when does the scene take place. A *Medium Shot* shows two or more people from their mid-leg to the top of their heads. This frame is good for scenes with lots of conversation, and it also helps show character relationships.

28 Video on Shooting.

A *Close-up* shows your subject from the top of their shoulders to the top of their head. This frame is what sets the film apart from theater and other forms of dramatic expression. With a Close-up, your performer is able to show emotion in a more natural fashion.

And lastly, we have the *Extreme Close-up*, which gets as close as possible to anything important you don't want your audience to miss. When a director uses an Extreme Close-up, they're saying, "Pay attention! This is important! Don't forget this!"

MASTER SHOT The master shot is usually the shot that has the entire scene in it. All the dialogue and action is captured in this shot.	**WIDE SHOT:** The master shots tend to be wide shots. This is where the camera is far away from the subject and you can see the whole person or landscape.
	MEDIUM SHOT: The master shot can also be a medium shot if your scene is really just a conversation between two people. Medium shots capture people from mid leg to the tops of their heads and are great for conversations.
COVERAGE SHOT Coverage shots include all the details you want to shoot in order to cut away from the Master Shot.	**CLOSE-UP SHOT:** Coverage usually takes the form of close-ups, where the camera is framing just the face of the actor. These are great for showing emotion.
	EXTREME CLOSE-UP: This is when the director wants to point out that this detail is very important.

CAMERA POSITIONS

Where you put the camera can evoke a certain emotion or response from your audience.

LOW CAMERA	Offers a different perspective. This could be a shot of someone's feet running away, or if the camera is low but tilting up, the subject will look very dominant.
CENTER	Tends to be the simplest and most benign camera angle.
HIGH	Offers a different perspective, and if the camera is high tilting down the subject will look diminutive.
BIRD'S-EYE VIEW	This is a shot where the camera is perpendicular to the ground, looking down.
POINT OF VIEW (POV)	The POV is when the camera takes on the point of view of a character, so other actors will look directly into the lens when they speak to that character. It also allows us to feel like we are really walking in the shoes of the POV character seeing what they see.
DOLLY	When the camera is on tracks. Used a lot for conversations. Track shooting allows the camera to move, but very smoothly and in a way that's not noticeable.
DRONE/CRANE/ STEADICAM	When the camera is mounted on a variety of different apparatus to give multiple angles and shots.
RACK FOCUS	When one part of the frame is in focus and the rest is out of focus.
PAN	When the camera is on a tripod and it pans from left to right or right to left.
TILT	When the camera is on a tripod and it tilts from up to down or down to up; good for reveals.
ZOOM (IN/OUT)	Usually done to show some drama.

Pro Tip! 180 degree rule! This is a screen direction rule that camera operators must follow. Imagine a line running through the axis of action (e.g., between two principal actors in a scene); the camera must not cross over that line. Otherwise, there is a distressing visual discontinuity and disorientation. If person A is on the right side of the frame and person B is on the left it must always stay that way.

THE PRODUCTION GAME

We like to play a production game before we start shooting that reinforces how to behave on set. Arrange everyone in a circle and have one person be the camera operator, one person be the director, and one person be the actor. Rotate everyone in class after each set up so each person can have a turn at each role.

The director should then give the actor and the camera person something to do. For example, if your class has a script about a rubber chicken that goes missing, maybe the director says to the actor, "Okay, I want you to say, 'Oh no, the rubber chicken is missing.' I want you to say it with a lot of fear in your voice, and camera operator, I want this close up." Now the camera operator has to move to get the close-up and the actor has to think about how they're going to say that line.

Once everyone knows what they're supposed to do, have the director say, "Quiet on the set." Then "Roll camera," at which point the cameraperson should press the record button.

Now, have your students wait a few seconds after pushing the record button before the director says, "Action!" This is because you want a **tail** for your edit. Once the director says, "Action," the actor should say her line.

Once the scene is finished, give it a couple of seconds before the director says, "Cut," to again give the scene a tail. That will conclude the scene.

Then, rotate students. Have the director sit out. The cameraperson will become the director. The actor will become the cameraperson, and a new person will come in as the actor. Again, the purpose of the game is to get everyone used to each role for a short amount of time and to learn how to behave on set. This gets everyone "doing," so they are comfortable when they start to shoot their own films.

CHAPTER 9

DOCUMENTARY PRODUCTION

Make sure that the scripts are completely written before the students move into production. It's sometimes helpful to have a table read with your students after the scripts are complete. A table read is a way for everybody to listen aloud to each other's films and to offer any help, feedback, or new facts—anything interesting that can help students make a more powerful film. You can do this on your class smartboard so the class can follow along. Once the films are accurate and have all the pertinent information, you can move on to production. In this chapter we will be going over how to record voice-over (which is the bedrock or skeleton for your students' films), how to conduct interviews, how to select shots and camera frames, filming B-roll, and how to use outsourced materials.

RECORDING VOICE-OVER

Recording the voice-over (VO) is the first part of production because the VO will become the main skeleton for the film: students will use this to help build their visuals and tell their story.

In order to record the VO, the first objective is to find a quiet space where students can take turns reading the script out loud into a recording device. Anything that clearly records sound or audio will work, including a smartphone or iPad. Students should place their mouth approximately six inches away from the microphone. Also, make sure that the device can send the audio file in the needed format to the computer you are using for editing. Nowadays, technology has created many different options for sending large audio files, including (but not limited to) Airdrop, beam, email, and even SMS. Most editing programs—such as iMovie or Final Cut Pro—also include a voice-over function and most computers have a built-in microphone.

VO can be captured in as many files as needed. It is not necessary for your narrator to flawlessly recite the entire VO script in one take. Record a separate file for each paragraph and don't let the students get discouraged if they make mistakes. They will have time to edit out "umms" or mispronounced words. If they ace the first two sentences but make a flub on sentence three, just start over from sentence three. This is show business! We can always "fix it in post," but keep in mind that the fewer mistakes to cut out, the faster the editing will go.

CONDUCTING INTERVIEWS

The second thing you're doing in production is conducting interviews. Interviews are a big part of Documentary film. Here are some tips for capturing the perfect interview:

Make sure that the subject is not centered in your shot. If you're doing an interview, you always want your subject to be to the left or to the right of center. This is counterintuitive, but it allows you to create a better depth of field with more interesting shots. Depth of field is when you see someone very clearly in the foreground and the background is a little blurry. It just gives the subject a little more texture and makes them pop out in the frame. If you can get some nice depth of field with good lighting, that is really a bonus. A lot of newer devices and cameras allow you to tap on the person's face and it actually

creates depth of field automatically. It's a really easy, fun trick to do with your students.

Have the interviewer positioned next to the lens so that the subject is looking just off camera. You do not want your subject staring directly into the camera unless it is a PSA or a strictly informational documentary. You want your subject to be engaged in a conversation with your interviewer. The eye line is slightly off the lens.

Have your subject put your question in their answer. The interviewer probably shouldn't be part of the interview, unless it's a style choice, so ask the subject to pose the question they are about to answer. For example, when asked, "Katie, what made you decide to be a journalist?", the subject should answer, "Well, I decided to become a journalist when…"

You always want your question in their answer, because ideally you're going to cut the question out during the editing process. This can be a tricky concept for your interviewee to get used to, so if they forget, feel free to ask them to repeat their answer: "That's great, can you say all of that again and use the question in your answer?"

> "You always want your question in their answer."

If two cameras are available, set one as a medium shot and the other as a close-up to allow for smoother transitions when cutting out parts of the interview. It's always really nice to have two cameras. It allows you to avoid using jump cuts. Jump cuts are when there is a very evident cut. You can often cover a jump cut with some B-roll or cut to the second camera.

Speaking of B-roll, don't forget to shoot some before or after your interview! Ideally, your interview would take place somewhere that relates to your interviewee (say, for example, their place of work) or to the topic of your documentary. Take some close up and panning shots of the surroundings to use as coverage when you edit the interview.

Pro Tip! In film and television production, B-roll is supplemental or alternative footage intercut with the main shot. The term A-roll, referring to the main footage, has fallen out of usage. These days, B-roll consists of anything, including all images and video, that you lay on top of the voice-over. It's anything that's going to help articulate what you're saying.

SHOTS AND CAMERA FRAMES

We talked a little bit about the ideal shots to use during an interview in Chapter 8. To recap, in an interview, you'll most likely only need to use Medium and Close-up frames. An interview is most likely the only place you'll use the zoom feature on your camera as well. With the zoom feature, you're able to get closer to your subject without disruption. A camera is naturally distracting, but a good interviewer should be able to make their subject forget the camera is there. If the camera is constantly moving from Wide to Close-up, your subject won't be able to focus on your questions. That's why the zoom feature helps; you can get close-ups without reminding your subject "you're on camera!"

LEVERAGING THIRD-PARTY FOOTAGE

It isn't always possible (or desirable) to use footage that your students have captured directly. Using additional resources, such as archival footage or fair-use images and videos, is a great way to add dimension as long as your students understand best practices. (See Chapter 4 for online resources.)

Using archival footage helps the viewer to understand the setting and timeframe of the film. For instance, if you're making a documentary film about waterways around New York City, you might look for unique archival footage from the 1920s that shows the city landscape as it used to be. You can use this film to contrast with the current landscape to demonstrate how your subject matter has changed over time.

Fair use B-roll and royalty-free music are content types you did not produce, but which you have the right to use without explicitly obtaining copyright permissions. Generally, violating copyright is not an issue with films intended purely for academic use, which is why it's important to explain to your students that these films can't be used to make money. If students do want to make films that could legally be monetized, they will need to obtain the rights to all music and imagery since fair use rules would no longer apply.

Ensure all students have access to all materials. Once your students find all the footage they need, they can upload everything to the shared cloud storage for the project or they can download it all directly to the computers they will be using for editing. Sometimes the editing and the finding of other assets and material can happen at the same time. We've had many instances where the students may be listening to their VO while editing and realize they need to find a completely different image or video. (See Chapter 11 for more on editing.)

SUMMARY

- **Record Voice-Over**
  - Find a quiet place to record the VO and be sure the recording device can easily transfer the file to the editing computer.

- **Conduct Interviews**
  - Make sure that the subject is *not* centered in your shot.
  - Have the interviewer positioned next to the lens so that the subject is looking just off camera.
  - Have your subject put your question in their answer.
  - If two cameras are available, set one as a medium shot and the other as a close-up.

- **Find B-Roll and Third-Party Material**
  - Find or create great B-roll.
  - Find archival footage and royalty-free music that complements your film.

CHAPTER 10
NARRATIVE PRODUCTION

After storyboards are done, your class is now ready to start filming! Shooting is fun but sometimes can feel a little out of control. If you can get an extra set of hands in the classroom, these are the days to do so. This chapter will outline how to manage your filming days, tips for capturing audio in noisy schools, and how to back up your students' work.

MANAGING FILMING DAYS

Go over respect and classroom rules again with your students, and make sure that if a group needs to film somewhere other than your classroom that they are accompanied by an adult. Ensure that everyone knows to hold the filming device or camera horizontally, not vertically, and to use tripods (if possible) for steady shots. Also refer back to Chapter 8 for the Production Game.

Assign specific production roles to students. In addition to actors for each piece, who will have already been cast by this point, you will need:

- **Director**: Calls the shots (where the camera should go and how it should behave) and directs the actors.
- **Camera person** (depending on equipment and size of groups, you may have more than one): In charge of setting up the camera how

the director wants it to be and making sure it's recording what the director wants to see.

- **Script supervisor**: Makes sure the film is capturing all of the dialogue written in the script and that no one misses a line. They also feed lines to the actors if necessary.

It's always good to rotate roles so everyone gets a chance to be the director, the camera person, and the script supervisor. Ideally, everybody will also have an acting role.

Review procedure. Before students begin filming, remind them of some essentials one last time:

- How to hold the equipment they'll be using: smartphones, tablets, cameras, GoPro, etc. Make sure they are holding the camera horizontally, unless they are making something specifically for social media.

- Etiquette on set: "Quiet on set, roll camera, action!" These words should be shouted by the Director to alert everyone around that they are about to start filming.

- Leave a "tail" for the editor: An actor should wait a few seconds after the director calls "action" before starting the scene, and the director should wait a few seconds after the end of the scene before calling "cut."

- Follow your storyboard: Film your master shot and get all of your coverage. If students are having trouble with their lines, shoot the close-ups and coverage while feeding them lines, then get your master later. This way they can be learning their lines for the wide shot when the scene needs to go smoothly.

TIPS FOR CAPTURING GREAT AUDIO

Make sure the room is quiet and the microphones are turned on and close to who or what you're recording, but not in the shot.

Audio is especially tricky in schools due to the amount of noise that is uncontrollable. Close-up shots can help ensure audio coverage of the master shot since they allow you to get the microphone closer to the subject. In a wide shot, it's really hard to get the microphone near someone's mouth without getting it in the shot (unless you're using a particularly loud mic or an additional, very sensitive, shotgun mic). If your school is comfortable with this, your students can also use their phones and the headphones that go along with their phones for recording. Attach headphones or a microphone to one of the actor's clothes and record the audio separately during wide shots. If you do this, the audio will have to be synched later in post-processing; there are many online tutorials on how to do this depending on the software you use.

BACKUPS AND DAILIES

While your students are filming you want them to look at their footage after each shoot ("dailies") and maintain two backups. Having them upload their footage directly to the editing computers is a great way to back up footage. It also gives them the opportunity to "watch their dailies" as they upload their footage at the end of each day.

When students watch what they shot that day, they can see what mistakes they've made. You can also help by giving them notes like, "Okay, tomorrow let's improve the audio," or by pointing out where they might be lacking coverage. You can also ask questions like, "What did we miss here? Why isn't the camera steady? Why weren't you using a tripod? *Should* you be using a tripod?" The goal is to get your students into the practice of uploading their footage and watching their dailies every single day. It should be noted that some software programs—WeVideo, iMovie, Final Cut Pro—save automatically. With that said, using your class's smartboard or projector to show your students how to actually use the tools within the software will be necessary.

SUMMARY

- **Managing Filming Days**
    - Assign specific production roles to students.
    - Review how to behave on set.

- **Capturing Good Audio**
    - Find quiet areas to shoot.
    - Get microphone as close as possible to the speaker.

- **Backups and Dailies**
    - Encourage your students to watch what they shot that day and back up their footage as they go.

ated to capture this variation; if PM2.5 is highly
PART 4
POST-PRODUCTION

CHAPTER 11
EDITING

When all the footage has been captured or acquired your class is now ready to edit. Until now, the material we've covered in this book should resemble things you already do as a teacher. By contrast, video editing might be something that is quite new to you. To teach it well and comfortably, you need to develop a certain level of personal skill. Fortunately, it is straightforward to do that using the video and written tutorials that are provided by the companies that supply your software, and by the many YouTubers who give their knowledge away for free.

In this chapter we will provide you with a conceptual overview for how to edit with your class. If you encounter something that is not clear, there will be some video illustrations on our LMS, but for the most part get used to Googling tutorials when you get stuck and encouraging your students to do the same. This is another time to lean on your student filmmakers; some of your students may have already mastered editing and can help teach the class when people get stuck.

Before you start! We recommend that you practice on your own by making three or more short videos and figuring out what might be difficult for your students. This doesn't need to take more than a few hours. Nothing will substitute for this, although you can postpone it if you have a colleague or student who can co-lead the editing parts of your course.

29 Video on Editing.

THE EDIT

Editing a film employs the same techniques as writing an essay or putting together a home improvement project. First, you assemble your materials. For film, that's your footage, your B-roll, your music and voice-overs. Then you need to put all your material/assets onto your editing computer via USB drives or the cloud unless your operating system takes care of this for you. And then you will import all those assets into your editing software, a process that is generally as simple as dragging and dropping.

The next step is a rough cut. From your imported library of material, you can select and copy and paste the parts you want into a timeline that will evolve into your final movie. This is essentially the same as editing with a word processor, except with video you have a time dimension.

Next you will refine and polish your film by fine editing the start ("in point") and the end ("out point") of each clip you have selected, adding the transitions (crossfades, dissolves), special effects, title cards, special effects, sound effects, VO, and music.

This should sound pretty easy, and for a basic film like the ones you will be doing in class, it actually is. On the other hand, as you might imagine, it can be as complicated and elaborate as you want.

All popular editing software programs have the same core functions. Here are some of them:

- **Cut, Copy, and Paste** are conceptually the same as in a word processor.

- **In Point and Out Point**: Learn how to adjust putting in points and out points into the raw footage. This way you're not dragging the entire clip (which could be very long) into your timeline. This allows you to work with and manipulate only the segments of the raw footage you want to use.

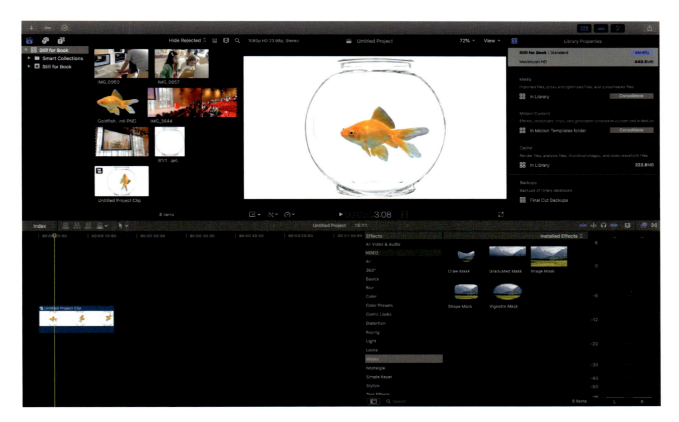

Example of editing software.

- **Dragging**: Not only do you drag footage into the timeline, you also drag music and enter transitions and title cards. This allows you to to flow and move things around in editing. You can also drag clips in your timelines to make them shorter or longer.

- **Zoom In/Out**: Zooming in and out allows you to get a finer detail on in points and out points. When you zoom in, you can sometimes hear or see where a mistake is.

- **Blade**: A blade was originally a tool analog film editors used to literally cut off what they didn't want in the filmstrip. The modern-day tool performs the same function digitally.

- **Edit > Insert Generator > Gap**: A gap is used for creating transitions or if you need some blank space or places to attach audio and video in the timeline. Being able to edit and insert a gap or a *generator* is especially helpful if you're using Final Cut Pro.

- **Generators**: Generators are other colors or movements. Generators are really fun to put underneath title cards.

- **The Ken Burns** effect for still images, especially for documentary films. This is the slow panning and zooming of a stationary image so that it is not stagnant.

- **Filters**: A filter changes the color, tint, texture, or effect of the actual clip. You can make your film look black and white, or look like it's an old film, or saturate the image with high color. If your film is supposed to be a little ominous, filters can darken it, or warm the image tone for fantasy.

- **Effects**: Effects are illusions that are traditionally added with a green screen in chroma key. Chroma keying is telling your computer to take a color (like bright green) that your actors are in front of and replace it with an alternative background. This is how TV personalities appear in front of weather maps, sport events, and the like. Using the keyer you can add explosions, fire, magic fairy dust—anything that's going to give your film a little bit more excitement.

- **Transition**: Transitions allow you to *noticeably* transition from one clip to another, such as dissolve, crossfade, fade to color, or a cube slip or flip. There are many transitions to choose from, and your students are going to want to play with these a lot.

- **Title Cards/Text Cards**: These are written effects that are especially useful if you're doing a silent film, need subtitles, or if you want to establish a date or location of a scene. Text cards can aid the audience in filling in missing pieces of the story. Your editing software will provide many text cards and title cards to choose from, though we do recommend staying away from 3D ones if you don't have high-processing speed computers. We also remind our students that there are many ways of making your title cards interesting and cool—as long as they're readable! Try to deter your students from picking fonts that are hard to read.

- **Music and Sound Effects**: You will use music (fading it in and out) and sound effects, like explosions, to help make the movie pop. Sound is such a big part of the experience when watching a film that you need to think of it as another element of the story.

DIVIDING TASKS

As in filming, it's important to divide tasks amongst the group so everyone has something to do in editing, while also moving the process along more quickly. Here is how we arrange our workflow with students, making sure everyone has an assignment. Be sure to rotate roles so that everyone gets the chance to contribute to the edit.

First, for Documentary one or two students clean up the audio and build the story of the film from the narration. Since the voice-over is the skeleton for the film it needs to be edited for any mistakes, e.g., "um" or "ahs." For Narrative, the first step is to put all the scenes in order with their master and coverage shots interwoven. While this is underway, the rest of the group can look for more B-roll and music. We like to have them set up a Google Drive folder where they can download high resolution images and videos and store them until the editors are ready to add them to the film.

Second (especially for Documentary), have your students start to put the B-roll into the timeline using the images and videos sourced by the group. For Narrative make sure all the audio is good and no reshoots need to happen. Once they have the rough assembly completed, then they can start to do the detailed editing, effects, etc.

Third, for Documentary have students add a Ken Burns effect where needed. This allows still images to have some motion; stagnant images in a documentary will bore your audience.

Finally, for both Documentary and Narrative, have your students add the music, title cards, filters, effects, and transitions.

The nice thing about editing is that you can have more than one editing team working with the same footage. This allows all the students to have their hands in the project, and it is educational and fun to see what the same footage can do or look like with different minds doing the editing. For instance, what one group makes into a comedy another might make into a horror film, all

depending on the effects and music they choose. The mantra we suggest you repeat to your students is: "There's no wrong way to edit." Play around, try new things; use variety in each scene. One of the scenes can be the master with a few coverage shots, or it can be entirely made up of coverage shots—it's up to the editors.

We like to do regular **mini-screenings** throughout the class to allow students to give notes, ideas, and feedback to one another. During these screenings of rough cuts, remind the students to give respectful and constructive feedback and to offer any and all ideas to help make all the films in the class better! This is a great opportunity for you to assess student progress and ensure the facts they are using are correct and substantiated. We use a spreadsheet (especially when there are more than two or three films in a class) to help us keep track of the groups and where they are in the process.

How do you know when your students are done editing? Give your students a deadline! As you can imagine, editing can go on forever, and while you want to give your students enough time to create a successful edit, you still need to provide them with a deadline and assess them based on what they could accomplish in that amount of time.

SUMMARY

- **Familiarize yourself with the editing software you will use with your students.**
    - Make a couple of short films on your own so you can learn the tools and functions of the editing software. Search online for tutorials when you get stuck.
    - At the outset, lean on your students or fellow teachers who know how to edit.
    - Try out all the different tools and functions so you can show your students new things!

- **Divide Tasks**
    - For Documentary, clean up the audio and find B-roll and music.
    - For Narrative, create a rough assembly of all the scenes and put them in order.
    - For both, add B-roll, effects, filters, transitions, and music.

- **Run mini-screenings to provide feedback along the way.**

- **Stick to a deadline!**

PART 5
MAXIMIZE YOUR IMPACT

CHAPTER 12
SHARING AND COMMUNITY IMPACT

While it's great to simply have completed work, it's also important to share that work. Here are some guidelines on how to conduct screenings, create impact campaigns, and use student films to promote action, empathy, and change.

CONDUCT A SCREENING

At the end of any film project, host a screening in a setting that promotes an active viewing experience. The screening not only promotes an environment where the students can celebrate the work that they've done, but it also gives them an opportunity to share everything that they've learned with one another.

Invite families and communities. Films are all about the audience and it's not about an audience of one. It's about an audience of *many*. You want your students' films to have a bigger impact, and the way you do that is by inviting as many people as possible. When you invite family, friends, and members of the school community, it is an opportunity for them to watch the films and appreciate what your students have learned, and critically, it is also an opportunity for your students to receive broader feedback.

This is also a great way to have a community event, to raise money if your school has a PTA, or to make announcements. In other words, it's a great time to come together. That's what all films are about, right? They're a time where we turn off the lights and we watch something collectively to have a shared experience.

Set up your space. For the best impact and experience set up the room properly. For example, make sure that you have good audio. The audio needs to reach the back of the room, so everyone can hear what they're about to experience. Make sure you have a great screen, maybe a smartboard, a Promethean board, a projector—whatever you need to make these projects come to life in the classroom. **Pro Tip!** Before the screening, be sure to test all the equipment with the actual films. It's no fun fixing it while you have a waiting audience.

Have the shorter students in the front—either on the floor or on slingback chairs—and then have the adults sit in classroom chairs. It all depends on your facilities. You want to set up the room in a way where people can come in and know that they're about to engage in a film.

This is a good time to hand out your rubric or note catcher. If the audience members want to be engaged in grading and assessing films, a rubric or a note catcher is helpful for them in assessing whether or not the goals were met.

Have the filmmaker introduce their film and do a Q&A. The audience loves it when each filmmaker or filmmaking team comes up and talks a little bit about the film before it runs. Have them explain why they chose the topic or what they were hoping to say. What was the process of making the film like? Once it is shown, do a proper Q&A. For this section, we recommend that you have a few prompt questions prepared for your students; you can even rehearse the answers with them ahead of time. Below are some examples:

- What was the most challenging part about making this movie?
- What was the easiest part about making this movie?
- What was the most fun part about making this movie?
- What was the biggest lesson you learned?
- What did you take away from this experience?
- How was it working with your team?
- How was it working in a group?
- Where do you see the impact of this film in the world?
- Who are you going to share this movie with?
- Is there an outlet—outside of this classroom—where we can share this film?

SHARE YOUR STUDENTS' FILMS

Films can die in a vacuum, but if they can get *out* into the world, they can create positive change, empowering young people to feel like they make a relevant difference.

Share the films on social media to create bigger impacts. Doing this is of course completely up to the discretion of the school and your community. A lot of schools have open policies when it comes to social media and some do not. YouTube is a great place to share the videos. Vimeo is another good one. You can also post to Instagram Stories or your Facebook page. This is a great way to engage with parents and allows them to see the work that their children are doing in class.

Create campaigns using the films as a calling card. If you want to go for a bigger impact, one possibility is to link your students' films with Change.org. This organization enables you to create petitions and it's a cool way to get your students engaged in the process of community impact and activism.

For example, Take Two worked with a group of sixth graders who were excited about brainstorming ways to fix the New York City sewer system. Collectively, they made an amazing documentary about why the sewage system is outdated and what flaws the sewer system has and what happens as a result of it being flawed. Their petition was to ask the Mayor of New York City to dedicate funds to fixing the New York City sewage system.

The students collected around 3,000 signatures. They asked the people who came to their screening to sign it. Then they wrote to newspapers. They really made sure the film was not the final product. They made the film be a *vehicle* to help propel their message forward and explain their position.

Promote positive culture in school. In working with your school's advisory board or leadership team, you can also have students create films that promote cultural or behavioral programs. Use the screenings to have talkbacks around your school's expectations.

SUMMARY

- Schedule a screening day.

- Set up the room and make sure all your tech is working.

- Hand out rubrics and/or note catchers to create an active viewing experience.

- Watch the films.

- Hold Q&A session.

- Share and create an impact!

CLOSING THOUGHTS

The idea that filmmaking and media comprehension are the third dimension of literacy is here to stay! You can simply look at your own consumption and argue that this medium may be one of our most powerful forms of communication, as it not only entertains but can change the hearts and minds of decision-makers. Teaching this in the classroom and encouraging students to communicate their own thoughts and ideas in this medium is no longer a nice-to-have, but a must-have in today's society. Engaging with film and media from an academic point of view enables your students to watch and create films critically and responsibly. Our hope is that when video is used by a skilled teacher in an academic context, this medium becomes generative, not passive, and builds personal integrity, encourages team building, and promotes more project-based learning.

We are not advocating for the abandonment of traditional literacy. On the contrary, what we are saying is that this is the natural extension and expansion of how we communicate with one another. The combination of all these communication tools, both new and old, will help us academically meet our students "where they are."

We hope that after reading this book you feel safe and comfortable adding filmmaking and media comprehension to your teaching repertoire. It's OK to be an amateur. The important thing is to expand your own knowledge within this medium and in doing so you will be empowering your students to use the third dimension of literacy to creatively tell their stories and share their thoughts in a universally understood way.

You will certainly encounter questions and problems, and when you do, please visit the Take Two LMS where our experts and community will help you. A substantial part of the LMS is open to the public. You'll find tutorials, classroom examples with actual teachers and students, illustrations, and a basic online course or two. We update the site a few times a month with new material. Together with this book, you should be well-equipped to bring the third dimension of literacy into your classroom.

*Remember: Video is fun, for them and for you.
Learn it together now and enjoy the ride ahead.*

GLOSSARY

1080P: A high-definition video format that displays 1,080 pixels vertically down a screen and 1,920 horizontally across it. "P" indicates that the image is displayed progressively, with each row of pixels appearing sequentially; video using this format displays a finished image to the viewer more quickly than the other video display type, called interlaced scan or "I".

180 Degree Rule: In cinematography, a rule holding that the camera should not cross over the invisible line connecting two actors in a shot in order to maintain their left/right orientation. If the camera crosses that axis so that the actors' positions on screen are reversed, it can distract or confuse the viewer.

24 Frames per Second (FPS): The rate at which standard video refreshes the image you see, meaning 24 frames or images are projected or displayed per second.

3-D: A filming technique that gives the appearance of a third dimension to a two-dimensional image. Either regular camera equipment is used to record the same images from two perspectives or they are generated digitally in post-production. A viewer then wears special glasses that allow the two perspectives to be perceived as one "stereoscopic" image with enhanced depth perception by the brain.

720P: A progressive high-definition video format that displays 720 pixels vertically and 1,280 pixels horizontally.

Act: A film's plot can often be divided into major parts of the story, or acts. The most common structure comprises three acts: a beginning, middle, and end.

Actor: A person portraying a character in a film.

Angle: Generally, how a shot is composed. This can refer to a camera's relative angle to the subject of a shot (e.g., high angle, bird's eye) or to the framing of a shot (e.g., wide angle, close-up).

Animation: A type of filmmaking that records progressive tiny changes in drawings, or in the placement of inanimate objects, one frame at a time in order to create the appearance of movement when the frames are played in sequence.

Antagonist: In traditional story structure, the person or force that stands in opposition to the main character (the protagonist), providing the central conflict for the story.

Boom Mic: A microphone mounted on a mechanical arm that can be extended close to actors while remaining out of the shot, i.e., by hovering above them.

B-roll: A broad term indicating any imagery considered secondary to the main recorded footage of the film. This can include additional recorded footage used to cover editing gaps in the main footage, still photographs, stock footage, etc.

Camera: Any device that records images. Traditional movie cameras record images on physical film, while modern video cameras record digitally. Cameras can range from small hand-held devices to large machines that must be mounted to either a stationary (e.g., tripod) or moveable (e.g., dolly, jib) framework for use.

Cameraperson: Anyone recording footage for use in a film, generally as instructed by either the film's director or director of cinematography.

Casting: The process of selecting actors to portray characters in a film.

Chroma Key: A photographic composition technique in which part of an image is replaced with a different image. Most commonly, this is used in conjunction with a "green screen": when actors are filmed against a solid green background, the green portion can be easily swapped out later for a different setting.

Climax: In traditional story structure, the height of conflict that represents a turning point for the protagonist. This is the most dramatic point of a film.

Close-up: A camera shot that provides a tight frame around the subject in order to show detail. A close-up of an actor's face is often used to emphasize or convey emotion.

Coverage: All of the footage a director uses to compose the final cut of a scene.

Crane Shot: A shot captured from a camera mounted on a crane, dolly, or other large framework.

Crossfade: A fade-in and fade-out effect in which one sound or image is gradually replaced with another, so that for a time they can both be perceived simultaneously.

Dailies: Raw footage which the director reviews at the end of each filming day to monitor progress.

Depth of Field: In photography, the plane of an image that appears in focus. A shallow depth of field yields a small area sharply in focus; this might be used for a portrait or to draw attention to a particular detail. Greater depth of field allows more of the image to appear in focus at once, useful for landscapes or to clearly show the background as well as the subject.

Director: The person in charge of executing the artistic and technical vision for a film by managing the cast and crew during filming, and the editing process in post-production.

Dirty Shot: A shot in which the main subject is de-emphasized, usually by including an out-of-focus physical intrusion like a door frame or another actor's body part, in order to give a sense of scale or of actors' distance from one another.

Dissolve: A film editing technique in which one image gradually disappears while another appears in its place.

Documentary: A non-fiction film with an educational, persuasive, or informational purpose.

Dolly: A camera mount that enables very smooth motion capture by being moved along a fixed track. A "dolly shot" can include vertical motion when the dolly is used in conjunction with a lever or crane.

Drone: A remote-operated device equipped with a camera in order to capture still or moving images. Drone photography allows for unique perspectives, such as birds-eye views, with minimal equipment.

DSLR (Digital Single-Lens Reflex) Camera: The most common variety of professional digital cameras, consisting of a core body that can be fitted with a variety of different lenses to meet specific photography needs.

Editor: The person who, in collaboration with the director, chooses which shots to display and in which order in order to create the final visual narrative for a film.

Export: A software command useful for changing file type or location.

Fade to Color: An image slowly disappearing as it is replaced by a color rather than by a new image.

Foil: A character in a story whose purpose is to highlight certain traits of the protagonist, usually by exhibiting the opposite or contrasting traits.

Hero's Journey: The archetype of a classic story: the main character experiences an adventure, involving conflict and ultimately personal change, in pursuit of a goal.

HD (High Definition): A screen with a high number of pixels. The higher the number of pixels in a display, the clearer the image. (See also 780p and 1080p.)

Inciting Incident: The event or moment towards the beginning of a plot that draws the protagonist into the central action of the story.

Ken Burns Effect: An effect of zooming in or out of a still image to give it more drama, a technique popularized by the American filmmaker Ken Burns.

Lavalier: A very small, usually wireless, microphone worn by an actor to record dialogue.

Medium Shot: A shot that shows individuals as well as some environment, usually framing an actor or actors from the waist up.

Pan: Motion captured by a smooth side-to-side camera movement.

Pitch: A summary of a proposed film whose purpose is to get producers or studios interested in financing the project so that a full screenplay can be developed.

Post-production: The final and often longest stage of film production, involving editing, audio-visual effects, and anything else necessary to prepare the film for release.

POV (Point of View): A shot in which the camera's angle is meant to represent what a character would be seeing through their own eyes.

Pre-production: The first stage of creating a film, including everything up to the shooting: developing the screenplay, acquiring resources, etc.

Production: The central stage of creating a film, namely, shooting the footage.

Production Value: The overall look and feel of a film created by the quality of the production, its props, scenery, costumes, etc.

Protagonist: The main character in a story.

Public Service Announcement (PSA): A film intended to raise awareness or support for, or educate the public about, a particular issue.

Rack Focus: The technique of changing the camera's focal point during a shot, which can be used to guide the viewer's eye to a particular detail or series of details in a scene.

Render: A software process that combines audio and visual elements into a finished digital video file.

Rough Cut: An initial version of a film in which the pieces are in place but more editing work, special effects, etc., must be done to produce the final cut.

SD Card: A small digital storage device commonly used to save data acquired by cameras, smartphones, and other devices.

Shotgun Mic: A microphone which excels at picking up sound directly in front of it while only faintly recording ambient sound. Often used to capture natural-sounding dialogue.

Slug Line: At the beginning of each scene of a screenplay, a line of abbreviated text providing the location and time of day for that scene.

Soundtrack: All of a film's audio elements, including everything from actor dialogue to sound effects.

Special Effects: Computer-generated changes to recorded footage, or physical illusions (e.g., makeup, smoke machines) that enhance a scene as it's being recorded.

Steady Cams: A framework for a camera that protects it from vibrations while in use, providing for smooth image capture without bulky machinery such as a dolly.

Storyboard: A visual outline for a scene or film that provides, in sequence, which shots will be used to capture the screenplay's action.

Three Point Lighting System: A standard technique of professional photography that uses three light sources to highlight the subject of a shot while minimizing shadows.

Tilt: A filming technique in which the camera "nods": it maintains its horizontal axis while moving along the vertical axis (up or down or diagonally).

Timeline: A common feature in video editing software that displays a project's frames in sequence, horizontally.

Transition: The change from one shot or scene to another. The visual effect of the change can be abrupt (e.g., cut, wipe) or gradual (e.g., fade, dissolve).

Treatment: A written summary of the story for a film, more detailed than the pitch but also used for marketing purposes or to get the project funded.

Tripod: A stable three-legged framework for supporting a camera.

Video Filters: A transparent or translucent substance placed in front of or behind a camera lens to distort the image, creating a particular effect as it is being recorded. Filters can be digitally created in most editing software.

VO (Voice-over): An audio track that provides informational narration, a character's internal dialogue, or other commentary in a film.

Wide Shot: A camera shot that shows both the subject and a full view of their environment.

Workflow: The sequence of steps required to bring a film from its earliest visualization stage to a polished final product.

XCU Extreme Close-up (also, ECU or XCU): A highly zoomed-in view used to bring out details in a shot (e.g., part of a face, one facet of an object).

Zoom: A shot that gives the appearance of moving closer to or farther away from the subject, although the camera itself remains in a fixed position (only the focal point of the lens changes).

SPECIAL THANKS

When I started Take Two, little did I imagine that one day, I'd be writing a book. Of course, I didn't make this journey alone. I would like to thank all of our incredible school partners for letting us experiment and play with them over the last ten-plus years; Matthew Brian Makar, who helped me see the vision for this work from the very start; Jason Santel, who is one of the kindest and best teachers I know, and whose effort and dedication really made this book a reality; Gio Gaynor for his brilliance, his creative mind, and for always pushing me towards perfection; and all of our other Take Two Teaching Artists—without you this work wouldn't exist.

I would also like to thank Rohitash Rao for the illustrations, Sophie Mathewson for the photography, and Katie Schloss for helping me get the first version of this down on paper. Thank you Abby Dudley for reading and giving me amazing notes, and the entire Weeva team for making this dream a reality.

I would also like to thank all my family and friends who support me daily: my mother Carolyn Kiefer for, well...everything; my father Charlie Kiefer for reading and rereading the book to help make it the best possible version of itself; my husband Eric Papa for believing in me; and my new daughter Sadie Lynn who brings so much joy to our lives.

This book is dedicated to all the teachers out there who are doing the work every day and making the world a better place for our children.

MADE WITH LOVE IN AUSTIN, TEXAS

At Weeva we care about preserving your memories, important life events, and memorable moments with family, friends and co-workers. Our goal is to create deeper connections and meaning between people by providing a platform that let's everyone share their favorite stories and memories while reading the contributions of others.

We excel at creating deeply personalized books for all reasons. We do the hard work of editing and design for you, so you can focus on what's most important: collecting memories. You manage the collection process, and we'll make your beautiful book.

Perfect for personal and family events such as birthdays, anniversaries, reunions, weddings, and exceptional for larger projects for companies, schools and organizations.

weeva.com